ORCHIDS
MONTH BY MONTH

ORCHIDS

MONTH BY MONTH

RALPH HANDCOCK
MARGARET SMITH

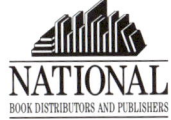

NATIONAL
BOOK DISTRIBUTORS AND PUBLISHERS

Acknowledgements

During this latest revision of *Orchids Month by Month* it has been of great assistance to have the advice of Graeme Banks, President of the Orchid Society of NSW Ltd, and also David Banks of Hills District Orchids and Don and Fae Jones, all orchid growers of many years' experience.

Additional chapters have been included in this new edition covering genera whose popularity has grown over recent years. The information for Chapters 4 and 13 was supplied by David Banks and for Chapters 6, 7 and 12 by Graeme Banks.

Facts gained from research carried out by New South Wales Agriculture and Fisheries have been included in the sections dealing with fungus diseases, orchid growing media and insect infestation.

For assistance in supplying photographs, sincere thanks go to: the Orchid Society of NSW Ltd; Warren Gray, photographer for all black and white and several colour photographs; Don and Fae Jones; and Alvin and Greg Bryant of Bryant's Nursery, Kurnell NSW, for making available the resources of their nursery.

Published by National Book Distributors
3/2 Aquatic Drive
Frenchs Forest, NSW, 2086, Australia
First published in 1967 by Dymock's Book Arcade Ltd
Second edition 1977
Reprinted 1981, 1990
Reprinted 1991 (Limp)
Text by Ralph Handcock and Margaret Smith
© Ralph Handcock and Margaret Smith
Printed in Singapore by Kyodo Printing Co. Pte Ltd.
Typesetting processed by Deblaere Typesetting Pty Ltd

National Library of Australia Cataloguing-in-Publication data

Handcock, R. (Ralph).
    Orchids month by month.

    3rd ed.
    Includes index.
    ISBN 1 875580 34 4

    1. Orchids. 2. Orchid culture—Australia. I. Smith, Margaret. II. Title.

635.93415

Front and back cover photographs © David Banks
Front cover background: D. Dorrigo 'Wisteria'
Front cover inset: P. Hausermans Candy
Back cover: Sarc. Fitzgeraldii

Contents

Foreword

The Orchid Society of New South Wales Ltd (OSNSW) is pleased to have been able to assist, in some small way, with this revision of *Orchids Month by Month*, a book that has admirably withstood the test of time and which has been the 'bible' for generations of orchid growers. The OSNSW was also able to assist with the recent revision of *You, Too, Can Grow Orchids* by the same authors. In conjunction these two books give an excellent coverage of the dos and don'ts of orchid growing.

Orchids are grown by thousands of people throughout all States of Australia, obviously with very wide differences in involvement and numbers grown. In New South Wales alone there are about sixty orchid societies. Many are in and around the Sydney Metropolitan Area and virtually every main centre on or close to the coast has a society to cater to the needs of local growers. There are also societies in inland areas such as Albury, Griffith, Canberra, Wagga Wagga and Tamworth.

The OSNSW is the parent body of these societies and assists them in many ways, not the least of which is the provision of judges for shows. The OSNSW is also involved in what is known as 'award judging' where the panel of judges assesses individual flowering plants and recognises those of superior quality. Quality awards include the Highly Commended Certificate (HCC), the Award of Merit (AM) and, the pinnacle for which all growers and hybridists aspire, the First Class Certificate (FCC). This latter award is not often given. It will be noted that many of the flowers pictured in this book have achieved these awards.

The advantages to be gained from membership of an orchid society are many and include access to library facilities, monthly newsletters, monthly plant competitions, plant sale tables, expert lecturers, plus the many social aspects that flow from a common interest. The secretary of the OSNSW, Miss Betty Oldfield, will be able to give the details of societies in your area, that is, where and when meetings are held. Her address is 61 Mountford Ave, Guildford NSW 2161, or phone (02) 632 5712.

The OSNSW is pleased to commend this book to all orchid growers—be they beginners, novices or long-term growers. There is considerable information of interest to them all.

Graeme Banks
President, OSNSW

Introduction

Orchids are perennials and many of our cultivated ones have definite seasonal rhythms that vary according to the genus or region to which they belong. In many instances these cyclic changes can be observed to occur during each month of the year. They do not, as a rule, take place suddenly, nor do they follow the calendar on a hard and fast timetable, for often seasons vary considerably. An experienced gardener knows the sowing, planting or dividing times by observing the bursting forth of the spring growth and blossoms, or the harvest time by the ripening of the fruit of the established plants around his locality.

Presented here is a month-by-month programme for orchid culture, which is mindful of these facts and has proved to be a most reliable guide. Each month the grower is reminded of the tasks requiring particular attention at that time and supplied with information which will be of assistance.

The more popular a genus, the more culture notes it receives. Thus, the fact that *Cymbidium* notes are most extensive, does not necessarily mean that it is of greatest importance, or that *Zygopetalum*, because it is discussed in just two pages requires only a correspondingly small amount of attention or should be relegated to a back

Sarcochilus falcatus 'Miriam Ann' HCC/NSW—a very popular Australian epiphyte known as the orange blossom orchid. (OSNSW)

bench and well-nigh forgotten. The true picture is that the cymbidiums are very easy to grow. The plants produce excellent crops of blooms in return for a minimum of attention, providing that general growing conditions are correct and the simple, easy cultural tasks are attended to at the correct times. There are available numerous hybrids that produce flowers from early autumn right through to late spring. Their flowers are very long lasting. These are some of the good reasons why they are so popular, even among experienced growers. Their culture notes may be, and often are, applied to other shadehouse genera, including *Zygopetalum*, growing in a temperate zone climate.

Zygopetalum plants are easy to grow and flower, when grown in conditions similar to those of the *Cymbidium*, and given regular and correct attention. The main reason why large numbers are not usually found in collections is that only a small variety is available. There is only a limited number of species worth cultivating and none of the hybrids are far removed from their parent plants. Their growing conditions are so like those of *Cymbidium* that most of the *Cymbidium* culture notes may be applied to *Zygopetalum* with complete success. Mention will be made of this again in the section devoted to *Zygopetalum*, where differences in growing requirements will be explained. What is said of the two genera mentioned applies also to some of the others listed.

Of course there will be some years when the seasons do not follow their normal patterns. Growers need to be observant and adjust their methods to take account of unseasonable weather, which may call for a variation from the norm. Because the reasons for providing certain conditions at various times of the year are carefully explained here, it will be simple for growers to make whatever alterations are necessary from one year to another.

You will enhance your chances of success as an orchid grower if you select carefully plants suitable to the conditions you can offer them. Give some thought to the climate of your locality. Many nurseries now label their plants as cool-growing, warm-growing or intermediate. By becoming familiar with the temperature range where you live and selecting your plants with care, you will avoid much disappointment.

Over the years, and as an increasing awareness of conservation and environmental issues has developed, there has been a definite swing away from the unnecessary use of insecticides and fungicides. Regular preventative spraying is now only practised by large nurseries, and then only under very specific controlled conditions, where the operators are totally protected from the sprays. The nurseries accept the need for such spraying because it is just not possible to monitor the plants closely to detect outbreaks.

The non-professional hobby grower does not have these same problems. Regular inspections will quickly locate problem spots and action can then be taken, hopefully without the need for application of sprays or dusts, which will be hazardous not only to the applicator but also to the general environment in which the collection is housed.

This revision has therefore removed the previous suggestions that regular preventative sprayings be undertaken. Every orchid grower, at some time, will have to apply some insecticide or fungicide. It is hoped all readers will be well aware of the dangers and will take care to ensure that they do not contaminate themselves or their surroundings.

May you find, as have many others before you, the joy and satisfaction to be obtained from your interest in orchids. Whether you specialise in one genus or follow several of the many paths along which this fascinating hobby can lead, you will be rewarded with a sense of achievement and you will meet many like-minded people along the way.

1. *Cattleya*

Very widely grown and easy to cultivate are orchids of the genus *Cattleya*. They display the loveliest colouring to be seen in almost any type of flower. The hybrids are more frequently chosen than the species, though many of the latter are worthy of inclusion in any collection.

The species are natives of Central or South America. They are epiphytes, found growing on trees or on moss-covered logs or rocks, in the humid jungles of the Amazon Valley and the other rivers in its locality. From these places they spread up the streams, along the foothills, up the spurs into the mountains where the air is clear and dry (not humid) and the temperature is about equal to that of the temperate zone.

Allied to the genus *Cattleya* are other genera of lesser importance which nevertheless are very lovely subjects. These include *Brassavola*, *Laelia*, and *Sophronitis*. They cross-pollinate onto the *Cattleya* or from one to the other. Thus, there is a group produced comprising genus *Cattleya*, bigenera *Brassocattleya*, *Laeliocattleya* and *Brassolaelia* and trigenera *Brassolaeliocattleya*, etc., with various requirements in regard to temperature. The flowers of many of the plants of this group are fragrant and come in a very wide colour range, in sizes ranging from less than 1 cm to more than 15 cm across. It is possible to select plants in such a way as to have flowers throughout the year. Because they can be grown in small pots, they are easily handled.

The whole of this group requires (except as far as temperature is concerned) similar cultural treatment so all will be placed under the one heading *(Cattleya)* for our monthly cultural notes here. Great care must be taken in selecting plants of this group if they are to be grown in a climate which differs from their natural one. Naturally exotic species, or hybrids developed from them, do best when being grown in their natural climate conditions (warmth and environment). Some plants, such as the species *Cattleya dowiana*, *C. mossiae*, *C. trianae* and the hybrids bred up from them, will thrive only in tropical warmth of not less than 13°C. Species *Cattleya mendelii*, *C. warscewiczii* (used much in early hybridising) and others must have an annual warm–cool, growing–resting period, without which they will not be successfully flowered. During the resting period watering should be kept to a minimum and potting mix should be allowed to dry out before evening to prevent root rot. For this reason a glass or fibreglass roof is an advantage for protection.

Some species, such as the above-mentioned ones or hybrids developed from them, *C. bowringiana* and other cool-growing species, and summer- or autumn-flowering plants of any of the cattleya group, will grow and flower quite well in unheated glasshouses in the milder areas around Sydney during most seasons. However, most plants of this group do occasionally need some extra winter warmth when being grown in such climates, to give the very best results.

Being epiphytes, plants of the cattleya group should be grown in one of the media recommended for such plants on page 38. Many of them make strong root growth and are vigorous growers so should be planted in fairly large pots. A strong, three-growth bulb division should be planted in a well-crocked 150 or 170 mm pot where it would be expected to remain for at least two years. Plastic pots will not need crocks. They need strong light throughout the daylight hours to bring them to a flowering stage, and an abundance of water while actively growing to make sturdy plants.

January

The plants should be in full active growth now and must be kept fully moist all the time. This means giving them abundant water every day during normal weather, if there is good drainage and a fresh, open growing medium. Try to boost air circulation inside a glasshouse. An electric fan will help considerably on still days. Vents should be open most of the time. Have them closed only if strong, drying winds are blowing or a sudden cool change sets in. Cattleyas, being tree dwellers in most instances, do not require the high humidity natural to the jungle floor. Sixty per cent humidity is quite enough for them. This is about average summer humidity for the New South Wales coast. High humidity is inclined to make them too succulent to produce large crops of choice blooms. It also encourages fungus growth that could be fatal to any tender cattleya plants being affected by it. Methods of dealing with this problem are discussed on pages 22–5. Visitors, air movement, animals, birds and insects all tend to carry and spread disease.

Fertilise the plants fortnightly, preferably with an organic and inorganic liquid fertiliser (see pages 46–8). A good rule to follow is that the thicker and firmer the leaves of a plant the less that plant takes to foliar feeding. As cattleya orchid leaves are both thick and firm they should be fed through the roots via the potting medium.

Many plants should be coming into bloom now. A day or two before the first buds open, plants carrying them should be moved to a cool, dry house where there is good ventilation and strong light. By this means firm, rich blooms will be produced that will last well and show very little, if any, sepal wilt (that is, sepals collapsing days before the rest of the bloom). Do not use overhead watering as buds and flowers should be kept dry at all times.

Brassolaeliocattleya Mt Sylvan 'Susan' HCC/NSW. Your favourite orchid nursery will be able to sell you seedlings with similar potential to this clone. (OSNSW)

Brassolaeliocattleya Ruth Purvis 'Magnificent' AM/NSW. Exhibition type cattleyas are always show stoppers. (OSNSW)

February

Plants will dry out quickly during normal February weather, especially if they are growing in a very open mixture. Keep plentiful supplies of water up to them. Keep fertilising the plants regularly. Several weak applications are better than less frequent strong doses, while the plants are receiving such plentiful supplies of water. Keep a watch on the repotting programme.

Reconditioning and Dividing Cattleya Plants

The repotting or the dividing of a cattleya plant is dependent upon a time in its growing cycle, rather than on the season. To explain: the butts of the roots of most cattleya plants hold the rhizome slightly above the surface of the growing medium. Also the bulbs are usually well spaced. With the advance of the longer days in early spring and the warmer weather, spring growth commences. The front eyes of last season's bulbs swell and eventually develop into new bulbs. As a new bulb grows, usually to about half its mature height, it starts sending out roots from near the base. The best time to recondition or to divide a cattleya plant is when these roots are first seen to start, very often during February.

   When reconditioning a plant try to clean most of the old growing medium away without damaging the roots too much. Move the plant into a pot one size larger and pack new mixture firmly among and around the roots, making sure not

11

to damage the young roots of the new bulb. When dividing, leave at least two mature bulbs with the new plant. The roots of cattleya plants last well if the growing medium remains 'sweet' all the time. If two bulbs are left with the new plant these divisions recover quickly and many of them will flower the following season.

When a division is made and cleaned up, by dusting with sulphur powder or treating with a pruning sealant, it should be planted near one side of the pot, with any active eye facing the other side. Plant it firmly but not deep. Stake all suspiciously loose plants and tie them securely. An ideal cutting instrument for severing the rhizome when dividing is a small sterilised hacksaw blade.

Naturally the plants will have had good growing conditions to bring them to correct dividing stage. The good growing conditions must be kept up to any newly reconditioned or divided plant, not just for a day or a week but right up until the new bulb, with its new roots, is fully matured. If this is done successfully this same new bulb will develop any buds which may be there and bring them up to good blooms at the right flowering time. Label new plants clearly with name, date and any other details which may be of future interest.

March

Watch carefully your watering programme for these plants from now on. A sudden cold snap can occur quite unexpectedly at this time of year. Much damage could be done to actively growing plants if the foliage is wet and the potting mixture is soggy when such a weather change takes place. From now on, until the spring weather arrives, it would be better to err on the dry side of watering and cease damping down entirely during this period, unless of course, the plants are being grown in a heated air-conditioned house. Fertilise actively growing plants.

Back-cutting, that is, severing the three front bulbs from the rest of the plant by cutting the rhizome through, should be done at any time from when the plant has finished flowering up to just before the next season's new growths start. Delayed back-cutting is always safer. The best time would be just as the new growth starts. Again a sterilised hacksaw blade can be used. It is about the best cutting instrument to use when back-cutting a cattleya whose rhizome is above the surface of its growing medium, and whose bulbs are well spaced. The back-cuts are left in the pot with the rest of the plant while they send out a new growth. They usually do this at about the same time as the leading portion of the plant starts growing. At the next reconditioning time they may be potted singly.

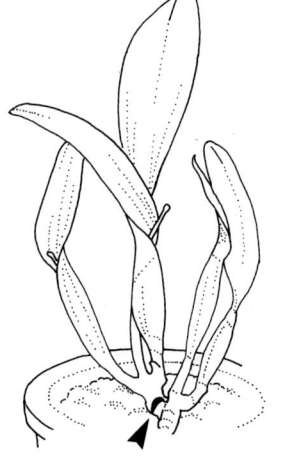

Back-cutting a cattleya.

Protecting Blooms from Moisture Condensation

March's chilly nights may cause flower spotting, through cold and moisture condensation, in unheated houses. Placing a light covering, such as clear plastic or even newspaper, just above any blooms needing protection during the night hours will help considerably to prevent this type of spotting. To hold the covering where desired use a round wire grid, say about 230 mm in diameter. Use the ends of the wire, which are left long enough and turned down, as legs to raise the grid to just above the foliage where the blooms needing protection are situated. As there will be only two ends for legs, a third leg may have to be fastened on the grid to keep it stable. It may be necessary to remove the covering, which is laid loosely on top of the grid, during the daytime, when watering is being done or when full light or good air circulation are needed. In unheated glasshouses try having some small vents open, top and bottom, day and night, to cause air movement. If air movement can be maintained most of the time, this type of flower spotting practically disappears.

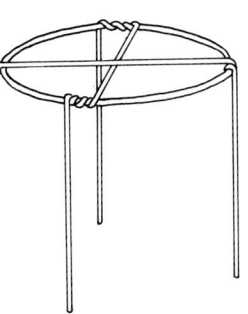

A wire grid.

April–May

Some plants will still be growing and some will have begun their rest period. Feed now only those plants growing in a glasshouse and those which have buds well formed but not flowered. Ease off watering, particularly in the case of plants growing in a moisture-retaining medium. Keep the mixture just damp. The plants may require some shade removed. If they are remaining damp for long periods take some shade off and increase air circulation. You can still repot heated glasshouse plants that need it. Do not let any sick plant struggle through the winter. Remove it and pot it up in a small pot filled with fresh, semi-coarse mixture. Pack a small amount of sphagnum moss or fine mixture around the butts of any leading bulbs of this plant to encourage root growth.

June–July

If you have not turned the heater on, get it going right away. Do not build up very high temperatures. Maintain just enough warmth to keep frost off the plants and off their house too. A temperature in the vicinity of 7°C is quite all right. On mild, sunny days have all vents wide open, unless experience proves that it cools the house down too much. If this is so, regulate the vent openings to obtain the desired condition; but remember that a regular change of air is essential for the good of the plants. Close most vents by mid-afternoon. Watch for insects or fungus diseases. If you can find a sunny spot which is sheltered from draughts, move the shadehouse cattleya plants there. Do not hesitate to hang some clear plastic around for protection for the plants. Keep the plants clean and tidy and have them ready for a good growing start next month. During the cooler months allow plants to dry out between waterings.

August

In localities where heated glasshouses are barely necessary for cattleyas, spring growing conditions will be detected in sheltered spots. If at all possible give plants growing in such localities a growing boost by raising the temperature to about 14°C minimum. This should provide better growths which should mature and flower earlier and produce bigger and better blooms. Also, the plants will have a better chance of finishing their flowering before the cold autumn weather sets in, thus making it hard to obtain good blooms without excellent housing conditions, much experience and considerable bother.

Keep a plentiful supply of water up to any plants growing in high artificial warmth. Such conditions tend to dry out the plants and the air, so damp down often (once or twice each day if necessary) to keep humidity up to at least 60 per cent most of the time. New growths will be evident on plants growing in warm positions during this month. New root tips or young roots will appear on the plants. If any of these are on a new growth, that plant is in excellent condition to repot or to divide, so check your plants and decide if any of them needs attention.

Start fertilising any plants showing signs of good growth. Cattleya plants usually have a sheath covering buds at the apex of flowering bulbs. The buds normally push

Laeliocattleya Chit Chat 'Lorna' CC/NSW—a 'cocktail type' cattleya. Easy to grow and very rewarding. (OSNSW)

Cattleya Summer Stars 'Melita'—a bifoliate cattleya popular for bridal bouquet work. The flower is of intermediate size. (Warren Gray)

Laeliocattleya Little Susie 'Fae Jones'. (Don Jones)

Brassolaeliocattleya Sylvia Fry 'Dundas' AM/NSW. Cattleya orchids are very rewarding although it takes a lot of tender loving care to get them to this standard. (OSNSW)

their way up through the sheath. Plants carrying bud sheaths with the buds not yet developed should have these sheaths removed. To do this, carefully split the sheath down into sections to its base and then cut each section off low down. Be careful in doing this not to damage the small, young buds there. Exposing the buds now can prevent the sweating off of buds in the sheaths, which may occur at this time of the season. Water cautiously those plants growing in cool, moisture-retaining houses.

The bulbs of cattleyas are usually trained to grow upright or in a particular direction. Attend to this task from now on, in particular during the active growing season. Straight stakes about 23–30 cm high made of 10 gauge galvanised wire are suitable to hold and train these bulbs.

September–November

Pay particular attention to light intensity during these months. A general rule with orchids is that the thicker and firmer the leaves the more light the plants will take. You will note that we recommend more shade for zygopetalums than for cymbidiums because their leaves are thinner and softer. We recommend more light for cattleyas than for cymbidiums because their leaves are thicker and firmer. In the case of cattleya plants they need only just enough covering to prevent sunburn on excessively hot days.

It is now spring and the amount of light per day increases; this must now be taken into consideration. If you do not have some form of mechanical shading such as blinds for the glasshouse, use the conventional whitewash or a good white paint. Take care not to overdo it. Apply a light coat at first then increase it as necessary. Remember, provide only enough shade to prevent sunburn. The heater should be off by now but watch for that late chill. If or when it comes, get the heater going right away as it would be disastrous to actively growing plants to check growth suddenly for even a few days. It may set the plants back a month for flowering.

Be alert for any sign of scale, red spider or fungus growth.

You should now be using a full watering programme. Do not let the plants dry out under any consideration, but do not water old mixtures to make and keep them soggy. If the atmosphere is dry, damp down regularly (daily) to keep sufficient humidity for the good of the plants.

Fertilise the plants for good results. Some potting materials will last in good condition for two or three seasons. Others break down in a season. Plants growing in long-lasting materials need more fertilising than those plants growing in materials that break down faster, as the breaking down of the organic materials being used releases food suitable for the plants. This can keep a plant in good condition as regards plant food without any additional fertiliser.

Keep in mind that spring is a good time to buy new plants from nurseries to allow them time to adjust to their new surroundings before winter.

December

The warm to hot weather cultural jobs such as watering, spraying or dusting, fertilising and especially air-conditioning (controlling the vent openings) must not be neglected now. The delights of having well-grown cattleya plants will be felt from now on, during the main flowering season, as many of the early summer-flowering varieties should now be in bloom or nearly so.

Most cattleya blooms have a lot of charm about them no matter what their colour, shape or size may be, but often this charm can be improved by small personal touches on the grower's part. For instance, having sheaths removed early from the flower stems will help considerably to strengthen them so that the blooms will be better presented.

Staking a stem will often show blooms to their best advantage. Where there are several flower stems on one plant or several blooms on one stem at the one time, stakes, or perhaps spreaders, are beneficial to place each stem or bloom in a desired position. Spreaders are pieces of firm, light cardboard fashioned to fit between the stem of the blooms to spread them apart where necessary.

Blooms whose petals droop forward can often have this fault fully corrected by using a pack of soft, dry tissue paper to press them back for two or three days when the blooms first open. Remove the pack when there is evidence that the bloom is set. Sometimes reclining the plant so that the bloom needing correction 'lies on its back' will be all that is necessary to correct the fault. Well-shaped blooms should be slightly cupped. Blooms which are naturally well-shaped will always be superior to those of lesser quality, no matter how skilfully they are handled. This principle is fairly general to blooms of all orchid genera. Orchids, like carnations, poppies and roses, respond to good cultivation, with personal touches.

There are innumerable opportunities to practise personal touches or individual initiative to improve any orchid collection. Often these may apply to one particular plant only. Should one plant be a weakling, as is often the case among any collection of plants for some unknown reason, take up the challenge to establish it as a first-class plant. Try various adjustments such as moving it to the other side of the bench or other end of the house, or perhaps raising or lowering it. Watch for results during the next several months or the next growing season.

In another case a plant may force itself up out of its pot, the roots holding the rhizome too high above the surface of the growing medium. A likely cause is that the mixture may be too tightly packed. If this seems to be the case loosen it slightly and add more mixture to raise the surface closer to the rhizome. The results achieved by providing individual plants with this extra attention bring much satisfaction.

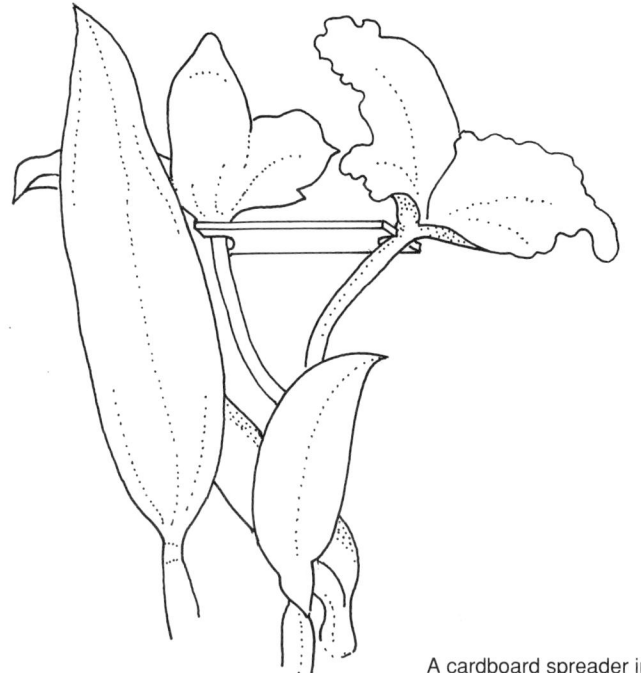

A cardboard spreader in position.

2. *Cymbidium*

No other orchids and few other cultivated plants will return such a wealth of blooms each year, for so little attention, as the cymbidiums. They are semi-terrestrial plants that are free-flowering, slow-growing and particularly free of diseases. They carry tall, arching inflorescences (spikes) of many long-lasting blooms and can be obtained in almost every colour and shade except black and blue. They are evergreen plants and their numerous, long, arching, strap-like green leaves always give their house a pleasing look.

Their culture is simple, but they resent overcrowding (a distance the width of a pot should be left between pots), need an abundance of fresh, free-circulating air, plenty of checkered sunlight (66 per cent Sydney light) and warmth. They are best suited for the temperate zone. Good air circulation may be assured by having benches clear of debris. Adequate ventilation must, of course, be provided.

These notes are intended for shadehouse conditions in a temperate zone, such as those found in Sydney, NSW.

January

Pay your orchid society membership fees! You will find it very much to your advantage to belong to one of these societies.

The first month of the year is a quiet one for cymbidium orchids. The only potting to be attended to is among the small plants such as started back-bulbs or seedlings. All cultivation such as weeding, and especially watering, must be attended to regularly. Well-kept plants will now be in one of their best growing months, so maintain your fertilising programme (see pages 46–8). Many new leads with their added foliage can easily crowd a bench. See to it that this does not happen. Always avoid overcrowding.

Watering

It may be as well to set out at the beginning the principles of watering, as right through the year doubts arise about it.

Cymbidiums will not flourish in a growing medium which is periodically completely dried out. On the other hand, they must not be kept saturated all the time. The best way to obtain a good even moisture is by frequent reconditioning of the plants into open, moisture-retaining mix (see pages 37–40) and by watering them at correct intervals.

Watering is dependent on the prevailing weather conditions, the layout of the orchid house itself, the time of the year and the condition of the soil. Windy days are usually more drying. Even in cloudy, damp weather, plants under glass will require extra attention when it is windy. When planning your orchid house, keep in mind that protection from the strongest prevailing winds is important. Watering of plants in a good open mix should be carried out thoroughly every second or third day, during calm, normal summer weather. On other days, a light sprinkling on top to wet the top centimetre of surface mix, and around the pots and benches, will give the continuous 'right through' uniformity of moisture. This is referred to as 'damping down'. During normal winter weather cut down watering by half and eliminate damping down. The weight of the pot is a good indicator of whether watering is required. The heavier the pot, the wetter the mix.

If using a fixed sprinkler system, make sure that the spread is even over all the

Spots of moisture have remained for too long on the leaves of these phalaenopsis, causing bacterial brown spot. Such problems can be avoided by ensuring that the green parts of the plant dry out within a reasonable time after wetting. (Warren Gray)

Slime, such as can be seen here, may appear after the use of chemical fertilisers when conditions are too wet. It will be necessary to repot. (Warren Gray)

plants. Arrange small pots and plants in front of the larger ones and watch that posts or other obstacles do not prevent water reaching where desired. In summer it would be advisable to hand water twice a week in case some plants are not receiving sufficient water from the sprinkler system. Hand watering may be done by using a garden hose fitted with a water breaker. These are available from most garden centres and give a gentle flow of water which will not damage even the most tender seedlings. Older, broken-down mixes should not be watered so frequently, perhaps only about half as often, but very thoroughly. Let there be a liberal run-off through the drainage holes. This could cut small channels down through the mix and let fresh air into the pot, which will do much to prevent sourness and will also prevent a build-up of salts which may cause considerable harm to the roots. All the same, beware of sogginess.

Too frequent watering of old broken-down compost will keep it soggy and turn it sour, a condition which will quickly damage the roots. They will turn black, first at the tips, and, should the adverse condition remain, root rot will start. With long-lasting sogginess the rot will travel into the bulb (or bulbs) eventually destroying the entire plant.

Black tips on the leaves, and root activity near the surface only, are signs that the compost is soggy and sour under the surface. Cold growing conditions will have a similar effect. Dull and shrivelled bulbs and leaves with brown tips are signs that growing conditions are too dry or hot, or both. These signs show up not only on cymbidiums and other orchid plants but on almost all plants.

No pot plant should be set onto a solid level surface. This would obstruct any drainage and air circulation through the bottom of the pot. Steel wire mesh is very popular now for covering benches. It is easy to keep clean and helps to prevent fungus diseases and rot from spreading. A 75 mm mesh is suitable for almost any pot. Another suggestion is to place the pots on slats fixed on a bench frame so as to allow spaces for free drainage from the pot. Heavy wire netting spread over the slats has the extra advantage of allowing pots of any size to be set onto them, in any position.

Where humidity is required, a few centimetres of broken-down coke breeze on a solid surface makes a good resting bed for pots. If pots are closely packed, this method is slightly warmer than an open bench. Should it be impossible to avoid a solid level surface, as in the case of a pot plant standing in a saucer, a simple remedy is to take three small flat stones or pieces of broken pot of the same size and so arrange them that the pot may rest on them. Try to raise the pot at least 6 mm or more from the flat surface. This will be sufficient in most instances for short periods.

Cymbidium Gurrana 'Marie' awaiting distribution at the Australian Orchid Growers Co-operative. (Warren Gray)

Cymbidium spikes carrying blooms of high quality, such as these, are carefully packed in boxes for export. (Warren Gray)

A section of the Australian Orchid Growers Co-operative at Mortdale NSW, which handles orchids from approximately eighty growers. Local florists are supplied with all kinds of orchids and cymbidium blooms are exported to six countries from June to October. (Warren Gray)

February

This is a month when plentiful supplies of water must be kept up to the plants. Not only does this supply the moisture requirements of the plant for healthy growing, but less sunburn will occur during heatwave conditions when the whole surroundings are moist and the plants full of moisture (sap).

In normal weather, water or damp down daily. During heatwave conditions at any time of the year water or damp down twice daily (that is, mornings and evenings). Try to keep humidity down, as cymbidium plants do not require humid conditions as do some of the other orchid genera. Flower spikes of very early cymbidiums may start to appear. At first it may be hard to tell the difference between a flower spike and a new growth, but a spike is usually rounder at the top. Also a lead is very firm while a spike is softer.

Summer pests such as red spider, members of the scale family, thrips and leaf-eating grubs are very active now (see pages 48–51). Keep the house free of any soft-leaved plants as they are the type which encourage most of these pests. Where show-bench or commercial cut blooms are being sought, a light top dressing of fowl manure, now available pelletised and deodorised, will benefit the plants so that they will produce bigger and better blooms. Scratch it into the top surface lightly, then cover with 1 cm of fresh potting mixture and keep the plant well watered for several days. This is to wash the manure into the mixture and also to stop burning. Root-bound plants may also be treated in a similar manner with good results.

Fungus Diseases

During the hot, humid days and nights, especially in enclosed areas where the humidity is usually higher than in the open garden, fungus diseases become very active. Give particular thought to these troublesome diseases before they appear.

Fungi that attack cymbidiums start from minute spores. They attack the plant through the roots, foliage and flowers, or bulbs. Last month's warning on over-watering should be heeded. The spores of the leaf-marking and the flower-spotting fungi require continued, prolonged moisture and correct warmth for incubation and development. Always try to avoid these conditions, by having a free circulation of fresh, clean air moving through the plants and benches, as well as by variation of temperature.

It is much better to attempt to prevent fungus diseases by avoiding the conditions which encourage them, than to rely too heavily on fungicides. Overuse of any sprays or dusts is not environmentally desirable. As well as this, there are some types of beneficial fungi which live in the roots and help in the nutrition of the plants. Too frequent, or too heavy, spraying will destroy them. When it is necessary to spray, wear a mask and protective clothing and start at one end of the shadehouse, walking backwards away from the spray. It is always better to spray in an open area rather than a closed one. When humidity is likely to be above 70 per cent for extended periods prevention against foliage and flower attacks is advisable, but care must be taken not to spray for the sake of spraying.

When a fungicide is used it should be spread on lightly and evenly either by spray or dust. After this application all overhead watering should be withheld for as long as possible. Most fungicides will take effect in an hour or so. They can remain effective for as long as two weeks and will help to control any new airborne attacks. It is not wise to apply a spray to a very dry plant. On the other hand, application of sprays to wet foliage has the effect of diluting the mixture and spoiling its balance. The best times for dusting would be in the still of the day when dew or watering moisture has run off leaving behind a damp (not wet) surface which will hold the dust. A good application of lime thrown under the benches helps to stop fungi spreading and keeps the surroundings sweet.

It may seem out of place to give now (in this month when no cymbidium blooms are about) the control measures to prevent flower spotting *(Botrytis)*, a name given to describe small watermarks which damage the flowers, mainly in the early spring, when the main crop is at its best. However, as the cause is a fungus, this is the appropriate place to mention it. Marks made by insect bites or other similar damage can easily be distinguished from the real troublemakers by close examination. The problem is caused by wet days and insufficient air movement. When the sun comes out and warms the plant, the watermarks will appear. Good air circulation will prevent this from happening. Install fans or position plants where there is plenty of air movement. Even a light infection is enough to spoil the flower, so control measures must aim at suppressing the disease.

When flower spotting is first noticed, fungus remedies should be applied. The same fungicide will protect both blooms and plants. The damage originates from miniature fungus growths, spread from the soil by water splash, that develop on various parts of orchids and other plants. As they are maturing they cause decay of the area where they develop. On cymbidium blooms the first evidence of this decay is in the form of greyish transparent marks, about 1.5 mm in diameter or a little larger, on the sepals and more noticeably on the petals. They show up most on the pastel colours and on tender blooms. The disease seems to be active when the temperature remains between 13 and 26°C and the humidity is constantly over 80 per cent.

A number of fungi, such as *Cercospora* and *Guignardia*, cause a condition known as leaf spot disease. This usually responds to fungicides and does not cause serious problems unless completely neglected. Sooty blotch and fly speck are also caused by fungi. They may be noticed when the temperature ranges from 13 to 26°C and severe attacks are experienced if leaves are allowed to remain wet for long periods. The longer the favourable conditions, the more severe the attack. Fungi incubate, develop, mature and spore (seed) after only a few favourable days. Each mature fungus growth releases many spores that can develop right away. If, owing to changes in the weather or control methods, the favourable conditions cease, these same spores can rest dormant, in good condition, for long periods, waiting for the return of suitable conditions for their development. As stated above, dry air, rise and fall of temperature and applications of a fungicide will stop them from developing or destroy them. When bread, cut pumpkin or other perishables develop mould, this is the time to use all methods in your possession to prevent fungus damage to your orchids, both blooms and plants.

To use a fungicide successfully means to cover the whole surface including the underside of the leaves (in the case of flower spotting, the buds and blooms) with a fungicide that will not cause damage or discolouration. For light-coloured blooms a light-coloured dust may be used and barely noticed. Dusts are generally safer to use than sprays as the latter have some form of buffers, spreaders, stickers, etc., mixed with them that may burn tender plant tissues. This burning is intensified where the sun's rays are allowed to shine on the freshly applied sprays. When using sprays it is better to apply them when the sun is low in the sky at evening or at any time on a cloudy day or in a shaded orchid house. Dust applied, then wet slightly, would have the same effect as a spray.

Should you change to an unfamiliar fungicide, mix and apply it strictly according to directions and then only to a small trial area, noting the effects after a few applications.

No doubt the best means of prevention is strict cleanliness, together with dry, airy conditions, and a rise and fall in temperature beyond the growing range for these types of fungi.

Fine organic dusts and/or insect specks on the surface of areas being attacked act as 'seed beds' that can assist the growth of the fungus spore. If the plants are at all dirty, force hose them to clean them. Any of the proprietary fungicides may be used on the plants with a reasonable amount of safety and good results if being used according to manufacturers' directions. There are some that will leave no noticeable residue on the plants after being applied. For appearance sake one of these may be desirable. Should any insect or fertiliser sprays or dusts be used, always be sure that these and the fungicide being used are compatible, even when used separately, several days apart.

Glomerella is of particular concern to cymbidium orchid growers when the eastern coast of Australia experiences a wet autumn. *Glomerella* occurs on the lower surface of the leaves and gives the leaves a brownish black or watery appearance. It may travel down to the bulbs turning them transparent. Extensive testing undertaken by New South Wales Agriculture and Fisheries has indicated that Bordeaux Mixture remains an effective control. This government department will give advice on making up and using Bordeaux Mixture and other suitable control methods. When using, special care should be taken to spray the undersides of the leaves.

Glomerella leaf blight has turned these leaves yellow, then brown. Infections begin on the lower surface of the leaf and develop in warm, moist conditions. (Warren Gray)

From at least December until winter, there is a need for growers, especially those with an extensive cymbidium collection, to be conscious of *Glomerella* and the devastating effect it can have on the plants. Continuing infections can be expected for up to two years. If the season is wet, preventative spraying will be necessary. As a general recommendation, where *Glomerella* is a problem, it is advisable, where possible, to grow cymbidiums in an area with a glass or plastic roof or with open sides, to spray regularly, to remove diseased leaves to prevent spread of infection and to grow resistant or semi-resistant varieties.

Several fungi can cause bulb rots, the main ones belonging to the fungus genera, *Pythium* and *Phytophthora*. These are related diseases which have, until recently, been particularly difficult to control. They are soil-inhabiting fungi which are greatly favoured by wet weather or overwatering.

When considering the control of fungus diseases in orchids, it should be remembered that the plants live in symbiosis with a number of fungi called mycorrhiza which inhabit the roots and aid in the nutrition of the plants without causing adverse effects. The overuse of some fungicides can upset these fungi, so care should be taken in the selection of the product as well as the frequency and rate of spraying. It is recommended that anyone requiring further information should contact New South Wales Agriculture and Fisheries at their Rydalmere, Sydney, office.

In open garden areas the humid months are the main times when fungus diseases appear. In glasshouses it is necessary to watch for them throughout the year.

It is worth noting that intermediate cymbidiums are less susceptible to fungus diseases than standards.

Cymbidium plants in bloom at Bryant's Nursery, Kurnell NSW. These are September-flowering cymbidiums raised for cut-flower production. (Warren Gray)

March

Watering during normal weather should be slightly reduced in comparison with summer watering. Damping down will cease from this month onwards until winter is over. On cold, cloudy days or cool evenings try not to water any of your orchid plants. If watering is absolutely necessary, keep the foliage dry. Still keep a check on the need to spray or dust if the weather has not cooled off and humidity is still high.

Leave all leads on back-bulbs until spring growth appears unless a glasshouse is available in which the bulbs can again be started and the leads themselves kept growing.

Many of the early-flowering varieties are now showing well-advanced flower spikes. Some buds will, by now, have left the sheath. Now is the time to take extra care in protecting them.

Control of Snails and Slugs

More cymbidium blooms are lost or ruined by snails or slugs than, perhaps, from all other causes. They will attack and do their destruction any time from when the spike is young, up until the time when the blooms are finished. They will also attack and destroy roots, young growths and other tender parts of the plant and generally reduce the flower crop.

Some of the first easily noticeable signs that snails or slugs have been around at night are: a spike that has a hole eaten into its side (sometimes eaten right through), ragged edges or brownish patches on the blooms, or slimy trails on the orchid house floor, pots or plants.

From this time on great care must be taken if the spikes and blooms are to be preserved from the ravages of these pests. One slug, in a night, can devour the tip of a newly started spike and thus finish it for all time. Should this slug not be stopped in its foraging expedition, it can and most certainly will go from plant to plant leaving behind a trail of devastation and damage.

Keep the house and surroundings free from plants or rubbish likely to harbour these pests. A popular form of trapping is to place wide, light palings or similar materials on any rough, damp, cool and shady place in or around the orchid house where these pests are likely to hide by day. They will crawl under these traps and it is an easy matter to turn these over during the day and dispose of the enemy by suitable means. Check the lips of plastic pots regularly as they provide good hiding places for pests.

Lay baits of one of the commercial snail and slug destroyers around under the benches. Do not, at any time, entice the pests onto the benches. An effective bait shelter can be made from a fully opened, empty, deep, 500 g or 750 g can. Simply flatten a quarter portion of the opening, letting this taper out to nothing at the bottom of the can. Place a small amount of bait in the back of this shelter where it will be kept dry, fresh and effective, even after numerous overhead waterings or a prolonged wet spell. Putting the bait in a can has the extra advantage of allowing you to move it from place to place.

An excellent all-weather bait can be made using the following ingredients (the proportions are measured by volume):

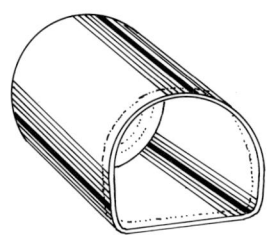

An effective bait shelter.

1 part	metaldehyde powder		1 part	hydrated lime
1 part	rice flower		3 parts	fresh portland cement
2 parts	bran			

26

All ingredients should be mixed and water added to made a thick creamy mass and then poured 1–2 cm deep into a flat-bottomed dish where it should be allowed to set thoroughly. Break small blocks off and place these under the benches or near the pests' daytime hideout.

Pure metaldehyde, dusted or sprayed, or snail and slug spray applied to the benches and pots, are other means of prevention, as, besides being stomach poisons, these are contact destroyers so will be lethal to marauders who may have managed to arrive this far unscathed. If their feeding course is also treated in the same manner their demise is certain.

As a final precaution place a cottonwool collar just under the first bud of the spike. Keep it dry and fluffy if it is to be effective. This will protect buds and blooms.

Autumn Reconditioning

Now is a very good time to attend to any plants left over from the main or spring dividing period, perhaps because they were very tender plants from an excessively shaded flowering house or because they were late flowering. They may have been overlooked for any of a number of other reasons.

However, the plants are still in one of their best growing months. They have had over the last several weeks an abundance of moisture, fertiliser, warmth and light (long days). The pots are full of young root tips. These (and indeed the whole plant) are very brittle. It would be wrong to withhold water to toughen a plant at this time of its growing season. Most of the spring growths by now have roots from 25 to 75 mm long. Should these be damaged they will die back and be lost. The new growth then would be without roots or at the most be able to grow only one or two before the winter dormant period sets in. This will result in a weakened plant with possible delayed flowering for the next year or two.

When dividing a plant great care must be exercised in breaking it into small groups of two or three bulbs. Avoid breaking back to singles in the autumn. Use pots just large enough to hold the plants comfortably, and a firm, moist (not wet) mix. When potted up, the plants should be placed in a shaded, warm place where they should be kept until re-established (three or four weeks). For the first two weeks watering should be withheld but leaves can be misted each day. The run-off will provide sufficient moisture. If the weather should be at all hot or drying, then damp down around the new plants twice daily.

A word of warning: It is not good to interfere with a plant from the time the buds have left the sheath until after the blooms are removed, as it can cause a failure to flower the following season.

April

Watering is reduced, and plants, during normal weather, may be safely left between waterings for four or five days at a time. Small pots and plants with fresh, open mix must be watered at shorter intervals. As the plants are now entering an almost dormant stage, any fertilising programme should be on a greatly reduced scale. In warm, glass shelters, top fertilising with some quick-acting, short-lasting fertiliser, strong in chemical urea, will benefit plants and fatten flowers, adding up to 12 mm to their width as well as purifying the colour. Fertilising plants now will also speed up growth, which in turn will shorten the life of the flowers.

Cymbidium Yowie Flame 'Krakatoa' HCC-AD/NSW. This clone has been recognised for both its good shape (HCC/NSW) and intense colour (AD/NSW). (OSNSW)

'Early pink lip' will be evident if heavy applications of high nitrogen top dressing manures or leaf-feeding liquid fertilisers are given at the incorrect times. 'Pink lip' normally occurs as the cymbidium bloom ages. The labellum gradually turns pink, the discolouration beginning at the hinge and spreading until the entire labellum is a bright rose pink. When this occurs prematurely, it is referred to as 'early pink lip'.

In the main, the correct time for fertilising flowering sized plants is from late spring to late summer. In this way the plants will receive the additional nourishment while in their best growing months and the effects will have worn off considerably by flowering time. A small number of modern hybrids are known to be susceptible to early pink lip. If you are growing for show bench or for the commercial cut flower trade, avoid these plants. Still air, high temperature or humidity, fungus attack to the pollen or dislodged pollen are also some of the lesser causes of early pink lip. Periods of very cold weather may be experienced during this month. When they set in there will be a noticeable increase in leaf-fall. The lower leaves of the older bulbs will turn yellow and fall at times. When only one or two leaves from each bulb fall at a time there is no need for alarm as this is quite natural even with the healthiest of plants.

A great many of the spikes are now stretching out and up. They must be trained while young to their correct flowering position. This is usually done by staking. Stakes are also used to support frail spikes and to prevent them from swinging and having their buds or flowers bruised or otherwise damaged. They are also used for supporting loose-growing plants.

Cymbidium Cronulla 'The Khan' AM/NSW—a superb flower well deserving of the high award achieved. (OSNSW)

Staking and Sterilising

The main thought when selecting material for a stake is that the finished article should be neat besides being suitable for the job. It must be strong enough to support the weight of a spike and its flowers, even when wet, and also thin or easily pointed in order to minimise root damage when driven into the soil and roots. Good stakes can be made by taking a length of 9 or 12 mm wood dowel, sharpened at one end. Paint the top 5 cm of the stake white, to make it conspicuous as a safety measure.

Another good stake-making material is wire. It has the advantage over wood in that it may be easily curved or bent to meet or set a spike. Always try to set a spike according to its habit. Never try to curve the top of a naturally upright one. Many of the decorative cymbidiums have tall semi-erect spikes that should curve naturally near the top, cascading the blooms in an effective manner. This type often needs correcting. This can easily be done by using a curved wire stake and securing the spike to it every 8 or 10 cm, if necessary. Wire, being stronger than wood dowelling, can be thinner (8 or 10 gauge wire is quite rigid enough to support tall and heavy spikes).

To make a stake with wire, cut off the required length, straighten it, then with pliers make a 4 cm deep × 2 cm wide 'U' bend at one end. Level with the short end of this bend make a 90-degree bend so that the 'U' lies horizontal. The 'U' is to act as a cradle for the spike to rest in. Where a stake is required to support a frail spike

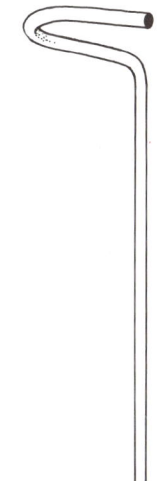

A wire stake.

it should be high enough to do so, up to the top flower if necessary, but never higher than it. This kind of spike may require tying at several points. In the case where a sturdy spike is growing in an undesirable direction or at an undesirable angle it can usually be corrected by using a much shorter stake. Simply set it firmly in position at the desired angle and place the spike in the 'U'.

Should individual flower stalks need correcting to show the blooms to better advantage this can often be done by means of a short spreader or maybe a stiff collar made from soft tin or lightweight lead. These should be removed when the part being corrected has thoroughly set. Wire stakes may be painted or, better still, covered with suitable plastic tubing.

A handy 'frame' stake for holding a spreading or top-heavy plant is one made of wire. Take a piece of wire whose length is equal to the width of the pot plus twice its depth. Measure back and mark from the ends the distance equal to the depth of the pot. Hold the length of wire horizontally, bend the ends down at the marked points. Fit the ends into the inside edge of the pot and push the frame-stake down onto the plant, so that the straight level top lies near any bulbs or leaves needing support. These are tied onto the level part of the frame. This type of stake can be made to suit pots of any size. It could also be made with longer legs to raise the level higher above the base of the plant.

Straight stakes, especially wire ones, are very dangerous. When searching through the foliage, as all growers do at times, one may easily be injured by the straight end of an almost invisible stake. Painting the tops of wooden stakes white or bending over the top of wire stakes will greatly reduce any risk of injury. When using a stake, select the place to drive it into the potting mixture, keeping away from the front of any leading bulbs or growths and from the edge of the pot as these are the most likely places for the young or active roots to be situated.

The tying of spikes and the grooming of their stalks or blooms should be done only during the warm hours of the day when they are less brittle, so there would be less risk of breaking. Very brittle parts of a plant can easily be accidentally snapped. When tying a spike, stand so that the stake is between you and the spike. Take a length of tying material and pass one end several centimetres through between the spike and the stake, bring it first towards you around the stake then loosely around the back of the spike. Continue around the stake and tie both ends together in a bow, not in a knot. If plastic-covered wire or 'twisties' are being used, all that is needed is to twist the ends firmly together instead of tying. The complete job should have a tight wrap around the stake and a loose loop around the spike.

When not in use, stakes, like pots and garden tools, should be collected, cleaned, sterilised and stored neatly away for future use. Great caution must be taken when using secondhand materials. They can be a means of carrying and spreading many diseases and pests and the ultimate enemy, viruses. Hollow stakes are typical offenders in this respect. Avoid stakes made from bamboo or materials with large open cracks, as they are very likely to spread disease from the soil that gathers in the hollows and crevices. As an alternative to staking, stems may be tied with strings to an overhead wire. The strings will need to be adjusted frequently to avoid damage to the spike. The use of spring-loaded, self-adjusting bobbins will save time.

To sterilise a stake, first clean it thoroughly. This is done either by washing it in several changes of clean water, or it may be cleaned while dry by scrubbing with a dry, hard, short-haired brush. When satisfactorily cleaned, treat it in a prolonged bath containing a strong solution for destroying fungi such as household bleach in the proportion of half a cup to a bucket of water. Wire stakes may be held over an open flame such as that provided by a Portagas torch. Secondhand pots, compost, etc., may be sterilised, however, the danger of contamination is so great that it is inadvisable to use them. Similarly, wooden stakes should not be reused. When working with cutting implements keep a small tin of methylated spirits nearby and place the instruments in it after each cut.

Virus Diseases

Contaminated equipment can easily spread virus diseases. Be alert to the first danger signs. Small black dots the size of a one cent piece may appear on the leaves. This is caused by a virus which will spread over the leaves and eventually kill the plant. There is no successful treatment for this. The plant must be burned to prevent the disease from spreading to other plants.

Mosaic is a very common disease of cymbidium orchids in New South Wales. The first symptoms are small yellow spots and streaks on the leaves. These later become more conspicuous with darker areas on top. The virus is transmitted by sap from infected orchids. These should be destroyed or at least grown well away from other orchids. Implements used on these plants should be sterilised after use and hands washed well after touching them.

Ring-spot virus *(Rhabdovirus)*. Affected plants should be destroyed. (Warren Gray)

Cymbidium (Snow Eagle × Palace Court). (Don Jones)

May

This is not a strenuous month in regard to cymbidium cultivation. A plant would have to be in very bad shape to make it necessary to repot or divide it now. Should it become absolutely necessary to recondition a plant it must be placed under shelter if rainy, cold weather sets in after the job. This applies right through to spring growth.

Wintry weather can be expected for the next twelve weeks or more. If the weather is dry and the wind moderate, watering should be slackened off to about half that of January, with no damping down in between.

Summer diseases and pests that are still about (mostly the scale family pests), will need harsh treatment now to be destroyed. Adult scale is destroyed by using one of the oil spray preparations. These must always be kept off all advanced spikes or buds and flowers. Sepal furl may be caused by applying oil or many other sprays and sometimes by wetting dusts already applied in the case of advanced spikes. In mild cases the sepals may only be slightly concave but in severe cases they may appear to be mere tubes. When applying any oil or other damaging spray to a plant do not allow a heavy run-off into the axil of the leaves or into the centre of young growths as this will cause burning. Any such burn markings may not show up until some time later, when they may not be associated with the real cause.

Only isolated, troublesome patches of either diseases or pests are treated at this time of the year. Fertilising should now cease until spring growth becomes very active and the bloom crop finished.

During this month some of the very early varieties are flowering and the buds of the main crop are showing. The average time-span from the appearance of buds to the opening of the flowers is approximately six weeks. Every effort should now be made to get the most pleasure from the maturing flower crop. As plants come into bloom they may be taken indoors where their beauty may be enjoyed for several days at a time. Avoid putting them into harsh conditions (too dry, hot, cold or draughty, etc.) that may damage either blooms or plants. Above all keep them away from areas where they may come in contact with any gas, motor exhaust fumes or kerosene heater fumes, household insect fumigants or sprays, and the like. Any of these will damage blooms and injure plants in only a few days. Some of them, in severe cases, will cause bud or flower drop in one evening and damage a plant beyond repair in one or two days.

Light Control for Colouring and Care of Blooms

As the buds emerge from their sheaths attention should be directed towards providing the correct degree of white light for the blooms of various colours. While doing this also place them where the blooms can be shown off to their best advantage. Have in mind as well the training of spikes (see pages 29–31). The colour of cymbidium blooms is often 'made' by giving different degrees of white light. By white light is meant the light obtained when the sun's rays shine onto thin, white, nearly transparent material or on glass painted lightly with white paint, allowing much light to pass through but cutting distinct shadows out.

Strong light intensifies strong colours. Heavy shade will bleach the pastel colours. Generally speaking all the red, brown and any other strong-coloured blooms should be given, in the bud stage, as much white light as possible, without causing sepal burn. Direct, strong, warm sunshine will cause any exposed parts of the sepals to become scorched giving that part a darker tone thus destroying the pure colour effect. Also it will cause the sepals to become reflected to such an

Cymbidium Sylvan Star 'Pink Veil'. This is very popular as a cut flower and pot plant. It flowers in June or July. (Warren Gray)

extent that it may spoil the shape of the blooms when open. Strong white light (not the direct rays of the sun) is given to spikes of buds that are expected to produce strong-coloured blooms.

To increase the effect place some form of shiny aluminium foil just under the buds in such a position that strong light reflects up onto the underside of them. This will give all flowers and all parts of the flower a uniformity of colour, when open. When a strong colour is made and the blooms on the spike are fully open, the roof covering should be adjusted to give more shade to 'hold' the colour. The pastel shades require less light. A slightly heavier coat of white paint or an additional strip of clear plastic or cheesecloth will be sufficient. Cream colours can be changed to attractive pastel greens with correct light control. Whites and greens should be shaded with some white material that gives a 50 per cent light to 'hold' the colour.

Always remember that deep, prolonged shade will alter growth and weaken the stem and substance of the flowers. It will have an adverse effect on the plant by weakening it to a degree that it may not flower the following season. One way to prevent this is by making a wire frame to fit loosely around the spike. This frame is covered with a porous, light-reducing material thus giving the blooms the extra shade while letting the plant have good light growing conditions. Make very sure that plenty of fresh, cool air will circulate around the blooms or severe spotting will occur.

Plants with pendulous spikes or those with all the buds facing towards one direction are best placed against a dark background to keep them in their position, with the correct lighting above and in front. Stand any plant with a pendulous spike high up so that the blooms, when open, can be viewed from the best angle. The plant with an upright spike should be placed so that the blooms are at about eye-level or perhaps a little higher. Any spikes that are intended for packing should be kept straight or only slightly arched near the end, not necessarily upright. A pendulous one may be set horizontally.

Correctly produced spikes are easier to pack than very arching or twisted ones. They will pack in a smaller space with less risk of damaging any blooms. Plants producing these spikes should be given the maximum of light that the colour can take without spoiling it and should always have plenty of dry, clean, fresh air circulating through them. When cut, soft, tender blooms will not keep as long as the hardier ones. When one of these spikes is carrying many buds, the top and any misplaced ones should be removed. In the case of spikes bearing more than fifteen buds, often the first ones are open and ageing before the last is open enough for cutting.

Too many blooms on a spike will also reduce the size of each one. From eight to fourteen blooms per spike seems to be the ideal. Fewer than eight would not be economical for the grower, while a number more than fourteen not only reduces the size but also gives less choice of variety of blooms for the purchaser. Disbudding is an accepted general practice with other plants in a gardener's care, whether they be fruit, vegetable or flower, tree or garden bedding plants. The removal of any buds or blooms from a spike whose blooms are to be judged for prizes on a show bench or for which an award is being sought, is forbidden. A whole weak (second or third) spike may be skilfully removed, right at its base, and no questions will be asked.

If removing a spike, treat the cut at the butt with an all-purpose dust and leave it exposed to the air for several hours before covering it over with some of the potting mixture. If a spike is removed early, when it is apparent that it will be a weakling, extra strength could be thrown into the remaining one, resulting in better blooms there. In other words leave on the plant the spike or spikes most likely to bear the best blooms. They need not be the ones with the most buds. There are no rules restricting light control for colouring.

The rules forbidding disbudding or manipulation of flowering plants which are entered for awards are reasonable as plants are valued and sold on their capability of producing a certain standard of bloom for the enthusiast grower. This is indicated by the awards they have had granted to them. Stating a

Cymbidium (Little Big Horn × Rod Stewart)—an intermediate type. (Don Jones)

minimum number of blooms per spike, on such genera as cymbidium or vanda and their like seems reasonable as it keeps them in their range of flowering ability.

Always try to place plants in their correct position before the spikes stretch out too far. Spikes, buds or blooms can easily be broken off or damaged if plants are being added to or taken from a packed flowering bench. It is annoying and unnecessary to damage a plant in any way through moving or transporting it. The surest ways of preventing any misfortune happening are: placing the plants in the desired position early; always having a clear place ready beforehand to receive any additional plants; and carrying a flowering plant correctly, that is, take hold of the pot about halfway down with both hands and rest it against your body with the top tilted slightly forward. This will cause the plant to hang slightly away from you where you can watch it easily. If you turn, the whole plant is carried around with you. Never hang a spike of buds or blooms over your shoulder while carrying.

Cymbidium blooms will last about 6–8 weeks on the plant and a little less if cut and placed in water with stems trimmed every few days. It is a good idea to remove spikes from the plant about a week after the last bud has opened, as they take nourishment from the plant. With the spikes removed, the plant will mature more quickly to assist the following year's flowering.

Bird, Grasshopper and Rat Pests

As rats may become troublesome this month they, and other pests not normally included in the list of orchid pests, will be mentioned at this time. This category includes birds that peck or eat buds or blooms; grasshoppers that chew the buds, blooms or any tender, green parts of the plant; and rats that burrow into the potting mixture, gnaw at the butts of the spikes or bulbs, and attack the buds and blooms for the pollen that they find there.

A flowering house should be made vermin-proof by having closely fitting doors and by having all vent openings covered with fine mesh wire. This will control birds and grasshoppers. Rats, however, will often find their way in somehow. They may burrow under the walls and come up through the floor or gnaw through weak places in a wall. They seem to be worse during cold, wet weather in the autumn and winter months, probably because of the shortage of their food supply, and also because they are in search of warmth and drier living sites than the rubbish tips to which they belong.

Always keep the orchid house area free of rats. Have several rat traps set in quiet, undisturbed corners; if baited with split pumpkin seeds or bacon rind they can be left unattended for up to a month at a time. Mice may 'steal' the bait so check for this occasionally. Always have rat poison in stock ready for any immediate need. Often one or several of the ingredients in the orchid pot will provide an enticement. Avoid keeping bones or very coarse bone meal, rice husks or anything of that type which may attract rats anywhere about the orchid house.

June

This is another quiet month as far as cultivation is concerned but much preparation should now be going on in the background, for next month it will be necessary to start the spring nursery jobs in real earnest; that is, dividing plants, reconditioning them or perhaps just arranging them from the flowering house into their growing or shade-house quarters. Perhaps extra space will be required, a bench may need repairing and other off-season jobs may be completed. Potting media should be laid down during this month so that they will be seasoned, ready for use when wanted. These are examples of the jobs that should be attended to and finished during this month.

Non-flowering plants in the shadehouse can safely be left without watering for a week at a time. Those in small pots, or flowering plants, especially those taken indoors or under dry glass shelters, must be watered every second or third day.

Watch out for any signs of slugs or snails. They should be one of the main concerns for the grower with flowering orchid plants.

Growing Media for Orchids

Now is a suitable time to get ready the season's potting media. Many people these days prefer to buy a ready-made commercial compost. For those who like to make their own, the following suggestions will be of interest.

When selecting materials a long-term plan is needed, as it is not advisable to be making alterations repeatedly through lack of supplies of chosen materials. The ingredients should be lightweight, long-lasting, plentiful, easily procurable, consistent in quality and, of course, reasonably inexpensive. Always endeavour to select local materials. Other than where specifically stated, orchids grow in some type of vegetable matter at different stages of decay. The mix should be able to maintain its physical properties for at least two years and should provide suitable support for the plants. As roots must be able to breathe, the medium must be open enough to provide good aeration and allow surplus water to drain away, but must also retain enough water to supply the plant's needs. An orchid mix should have a pH factor in the range of 5.0 to 6.5, that is, it should be slightly acid.

Where exposed materials such as leaf-mould, tree bark, fern fibre, etc., are gathered from the vicinity of cities, large towns or thickly populated areas, where birds or animals move freely from domestic gardens to the source of materials, they should be sterilised. Passing steam through the materials until the temperature at the centre rises to at least 85°C is quite an effective method. Small quantities could be placed in a clean drum or an old copper and covered with water, which is brought to the boil. A soil fumigant that destroys soil-borne fungus diseases and insects could be used but caution should be taken when using one of these. Use it some considerable time before the materials are needed.

After the mix or any of its ingredients is sterilised with a fumigant, turn and aerate it several times before using it. Then use a sample in one or two pots of orchids only. After about a month knock the plants out of these pots, shake the medium away and check on the roots and plants to see how they have been affected and whether the medium is safe to use. Heed that old orchid growers' saying, 'Hasten slowly.' This applies to any experimentation.

It is not good to sterilise all ingredients each time before using them as this would leave the mix 'dead' by killing all bacteria.

Orchids may be divided into various categories according to their growing habit. Suitable growing media and mixes for each category are as follows:

Epiphytes

These are genera that grow on the outer bark of trees or other plants, moss-covered logs or rocks (for example, *Cattleya*, *Dendrobium*). These plants must have

The aerial roots of epiphytic species can be seen in this group of dendrobiums. (Warren Gray)

continuous fresh air around their roots, and while actively growing must be kept fully moist. Some have an almost dormant period; these should then be kept quite dry. (For advice in these cases watch our monthly notes.) These conditions are best obtained by using a growing medium made from coarse lumps of bark, which may be reinforced with charcoal or fine crocks, with the dust removed with a 6 mm mesh sieve. A semi-terrestrial compost with the fine particles removed with the same size mesh sieve, could also be used. Any of these can be watered daily without risk of sogginess or sourness. Always try to use materials that will last for at least two years.

Semi-terrestrials

These include (1) the type that grow sometimes in decayed hollows of trees where there is a mixture of rotted wood, leaves, etc., at different stages of decay (for example, *Cymbidium*), and (2) the type which grow in the decaying vegetable matter at the butts of trees or in pockets on rocky cliffs (for example, *Paphiopedilum*). The ingredients for a growing medium for these should have the same long-lasting qualities as that for epiphytes but should have the large crevices filled with finer particles.

Materials that may be freely used are sterile, coarse leaf-mould, long-lasting seasoned wood shavings, pine bark, peat moss, peanut shells, charcoal, treefern fibre, polystyrene, scoria, perlite, sand, pumice, vermiculite or any similar materials (see chart on page 40).

A growing medium which has proved successful for many years for a large section of semi-terrestrial type orchids can be made by using the following ingredients (the proportions are measured by volume):

200 parts   seasoned, long-lasting wood shavings. (To season, level a heap
over to a depth of about 1 metre. Weather with at least 600 mm of

38

	rain or by sprinklers, at intervals, over a period of at least six months.)
100 parts	pine bark
50 parts	sharp sand
12 parts	fresh fowl manure
1 part	blood and bone fertiliser
1 part	complete garden fertiliser, strong in phosphoric acid

Thoroughly mix all ingredients, then dampen, leave five days, turn them over, then leave a further five days before using. For storing, keep the mixture moist but covered, to protect from heavy rains. Turn occasionally to keep fresh. This mix has sufficient correctly balanced plant food, immediately available, to grow strong, healthy orchid plants through all stages on to flowering. In addition it is moisture-retaining and will take much water, while new, without risk of sogginess or sourness. It will last, in good condition, for about two years. Many growers now disagree with including nutrients in the mix. Those who hold this view believe that it is easier to control the application of fertilisers if the orchid mix has a low natural fertility. By experimentation growers can determine the approach most successful for them.

Terrestrials

These are the plants growing completely in the ground (for example, *Phaius*, *Bletia*). They are grown preferably in a sandy loam rich in humus.

Cymbidium Pharaoh Gold 'John's Delight'. (Don Jones)

A Comparison of Various Media Ingredients

Medium	Aeration	Water-holding capacity	pH	Advantages	Disadvantages	Comments
Pine bark	Excellent	Good			May prevent nitrogen from reaching plants	Before use it should be stored in a moist heap for at least six months to avoid toxicity
Good quality spaghnum peatmoss	Good	Excellent	Low	Is slow to decompose	May be expensive	
Scoria		Poor	High	Is lightweight	High pH may cause iron deficiency	
Sand	Good	Poor			Sand is heavy and has no nutrient-holding ability. Most supply sources are contaminated so sterilising is essential	Do not use beach sand. Coarse river sand is best. The smaller the size of sand particles, the better the water-holding capacity
Pumice	Better than sand	Better than sand		Comparatively cheap. Lighter than sand	No nutrient-holding ability	
Perlite	Good	Excellent		Lightweight	No nutrient-holding ability	
Vermiculite	Better than perlite	High	High	Lightweight. Contains some nutrients including potassium and magnesium	Can become soggy if too high a content in the mix	
Soil	Aeration decreases as it compacts	Compacts in containers and becomes waterlogged		Excellent nutrient-holding capacity	Varies in quality and often contaminated	Do not use
Compost and Leaf-mould	Aeration decreases as medium breaks down	Good		Good nutrient-holding capacity	May be contaminated. Will need to be sterilised	

July

There should be considerable activity in the cymbidium house this month. Plants that are flowering or starting to show buds cannot be neglected for one day if the flower crop is valued. These plants should be kept reasonably moist at their roots at all times, even during cool, damp weather. Although they may not appear to be actively growing, moisture is passing through them. If they are allowed to dry out the blooms will suffer. The first sign of dryness will appear in the sheaths along the spike which will start to brown off. Non-flowering plants may still be left slightly on the dry side. Ants, aphids, slugs and snails, rats, in fact pests of all kinds, seem to be lurking in every part of the house, ready to attack at any opportune moment. Beat them to it.

Keep the house clean of anything that may entice any one of these pests. Lay ant, slug or rat bait, whichever is necessary.

Rain or rough weather can quickly damage flowers and shorten their freshness. Protect them from these elements by housing all flowering plants under some kind of roofing or, where this is not practicable, cover them with clear plastic during any rough weather. Many spikes are lengthening fast and those that have been staked and need tying must be attended to every few days to prevent misshapen spikes. As the blooms of the early-flowering plants fade they should be removed from the plants, which should then be prepared for the next twelve months, perhaps by repotting or dividing. Some growers prefer to postpone breaking up of early-flowering plants until September when a spike would already have begun to form.

Dividing Cymbidium Plants

Cymbidium orchids, like other plants, originally start from seed. A seedling develops leaves from a short pear-shaped stem called a pseudobulb. 'Pseudo' means 'sham' or 'false'. In conformity with the usual practice of growers, in these pages the pseudobulb will be referred to as 'bulb' only. Behind the base of each leaf is an eye. As the seedling ages and matures one or more of these eyes develop to new growths. A new growth matures in a season (year) and is ready to carry on again. In this way new growths are produced each year. Each successive growth being 'mothered' by the older bulb (or bulbs) should get stronger and larger until it reaches a stage where it is strong and mature enough to flower. This may take four successive seasons, less in ideal growing conditions and, of course, more in adverse ones. By the time a seedling has grown to flowering size it may have several bulbs at different stages. Each stage of the bulb's development has a special name by which it is generally known. These are:

1. the *lead*, which is a well-established growth with a good root system but which has not bulbed out;
2. the *leading bulb*, the last bulb made, which has an active lead coming away from it;
3. the *swinger* or *waning bulb*, which has some live roots and some green leaves; and
4. the *back-bulbs*, which are devoid of both roots and leaves.

When a cymbidium has all these bulbs it is time to consider dividing it. Other factors to be taken into consideration are:

1. keeping the plant 'young'—no cymbidium plant should be left unattended when it has a number of back-bulbs in its centre;
2. getting the maximum flowering from the plant while keeping it within a desired size range; and
3. the season, growing stage and condition of the plant.

Cymbidiums can be divided at any time of the year except in the hottest or coldest months. It is important first to check that the tips of the roots are showing a healthy white colouration and that the weather is such that it will encourage growth. Although breaking up has traditionally followed flowering, this is not necessarily the best plan, as the roots are not active at this time. It is a good plan to wait about two months after flowering, especially in the case of early-flowering varieties.

1

2

3

4

5

6

7

Dividing Plants

1. This plant needs dividing, preferably in September. (Warren Gray)

2. Healthy white tips on the roots indicate that this cymbidium plant ready for repotting or breaking up. These tips usually appear two to three months after winter ends. Shake the old mix out. Cut through the root about 50 mm from the bottom. If dividing, look for a weak spot. Crack the plant apart. Cut through with a sterilised knife. (Warren Gray)

3. Remove the old back-bulbs, trim their old roots and remove their leave to stop infestation with mealy bug or scale. (Warren Gray)

4. Keep intact the forward part of the plant; that is, the part with the new leads. It is usual to leave three growths. (Warren Gray)

5. Separate the plant into two or more pieces, each with three bulbs wher possible. (Warren Gray)

6. Seal cuts on divisions with a pruning sealant. (Warren Gray)

7. When potting up, it is important to position the plant correctly. While filling the pot with compost, hold the green bulb so that the base of the bul is level with the top of the pot. Shake the pot gently while filling. Keep th cut side of the plant to the back of the pot to allow room for all the new growths to form. Label the plant. The back-bulbs are planted in small pot or, if there are several of the same kind, they can be planted in a large po or small deep seed box. (Warren Gray)

Potting on should be done when the roots curl around the bottom of the pot and before they get too tight. The plant should be moved into a pot large enough to allow about 2 cm around the plant. If the plant has been left too long and the roots have become too tight, tease them apart a little, as this helps the new roots to grow into the potting mix. If the plant becomes rootbound and tight, cut the bottom 5 cm off the roots, place the plant in a bucket of water and allow it to soak, then crack the plant where it breaks readily and the roots will come apart easily. Try to keep intact the forward part of the plant, that is, the part with the new leads, as this will give you the flowering plant for the next year. Remove all roots from the old back-bulbs.

Cutting instruments should first be sterilised by immersing in a sterilising solution or holding over an open flame. In the case of the other divisions any damaged roots should be removed where the damage nearest the bulb occurs. If the plant is not potbound, separate it into two or more pieces each with three bulbs where possible.

The new plants are laid in a cool, airy place with all the butts facing the one way. While here the roots and any broken parts are dusted with a fungicide, such as Bordeaux Mixture or an all-purpose dust. It is beneficial to leave the plants there for about half an hour for all the cut or bruised parts to seal themselves. A normal pruning sealant may be used, such as sulphur or tar. After this each division is planted into as small a pot as will comfortably hold it. The most suitable pots are those made of soft black plastic. The 200 and 250 mm pots should have extra holes punched into the base, but this is not necessary for the smaller sizes. When planting, just moisten and firm the mix, do not ram it tightly. Build up some mix

Cymbidium (Minneken × Baltic)—an intermediate type. (Don Jones)

slightly around the bulbs of the new plant. This will temporarily support them and it will keep them moist and cool thus doing much to prevent bulb shrinkage. The mix will settle down or level off by the time the plant becomes established. Then it should be about level with the bottom of the bulbs, which should be about 1 cm down in the pot.

Any really loose plants should be staked and tied. Each new plant should be labelled with its correct name. In a case where a name has been lost, label all divisions of that plant with the same identification number or letter. Do not give it a fanciful name as all orchid names should be registered. Also never give a variety name to some part of a plant. Only where you have all the clone under control, may you be privileged to give it a variety name. Put the new plants in a warm, shaded position in the house.

Do not water for at least two weeks unless the weather is very hot, in which case the leaves can be misted. When they are established they can be treated the same as the other established plants.

If a high-quality plant is divided, all the bulbs should be used for propagation. The back-bulbs, in this case, are cleaned and planted to about one-third of their depth in damp sawdust or coarse river sand either in small pots or, where there are several of the one kind, they may all be planted in a large pot or a small, deep seed box.

They are started in a warm, just damp, shady position. They are periodically examined and when an eye is observed to develop to the size of a grain of wheat, that bulb is lifted to bring the eye near the surface of the sawdust. When roots are seen to start in any growth, the bulb carrying it is moved into adult cymbidium mix but still kept in the nursery part of the house.

A bulb or back-bulb may be used for propagation several times. When a growth has reached a stage where it appears strong and has several leaves and roots it can be removed from the bulb and potted up separately. The growth is kept in the nursery part where it will soon establish itself.

The bulb is again planted where it usually starts another growth that can also be removed at the correct stage. Sometimes the same bulb will start four or more growths either singly or in pairs or bigger groups. Each time a bulb starts a growth its vitality lessens and the growths get weaker, taking longer to grow to flowering size plants.

August

In the open garden signs of spring will be in evidence, so likewise, there will be spring movement among the orchids even though it may not be very apparent. Keep right up with reconditioning or dividing of plants as the blooms are removed. As early-flowering plants become established after dividing, etc., spring cultivation should be commenced by watering them every third or fourth day and giving them all the natural warmth available, plenty of light and fresh air. The main crop of blooms is now coming up to their best. Heed last month's advice on watering of flowering plants. Remember compost will dry out faster now than then and, as this is usually a windy month, extra care must be taken to prevent any shortening of the life or freshness of the blooms through lack of moisture. Watering of all plants will be stepped up during this month but no damping down is yet required.

Spring orchid shows are now being held. These are organised to encourage amateur growers to show their plants and to promote orchids to the public.

Preparing Plants for Shows

A little pre-show attention on the plant owner's part performs wonders. Even if no prize is won, a well-groomed plant will make its owner proud. When the plants are returned home they should not have been unduly damaged. Often these shows are held in halls or shopping centres where growing conditions are not always the best. Usually most damage is done to plants through lack of moisture. As a rule, hall or centre owners will not permit water to drip from the pot plants onto the floors for fear of staining or otherwise damaging them. If a show lasts for three or more days, be very sure to water all plants to saturation point on the morning of entering them. To further assist retention of moisture loosen the surface of the mix and cover it with some sort of neat, damp, moisture-retaining materials such as peat, sphagnum or some other moss, coarse pine bark or seasoned wood shavings.

While attending to the moisture requirements of the plant it is a good time to clean and tidy it up. Trim off any old leaves or dead leaf tips, or any disfigured parts of the plant. Remove all dry husks from the bulbs and spikes. If any of these are obstinate they can easily be removed by taking them off in layers, starting from the bottom of the bulb and by splitting them down the leaf grain and removing them in sections. Wash the leaves and finally the entire plant. Plants on show benches should be well groomed in addition to being well grown and flowered.

September

This is the cymbidium growers' month. Well-grown and well-flowered 'main crop' plants are now about at their best. Admiring these lovely things, attending shows, visiting other enthusiasts' collections or receiving visitors are many of the activities crammed into this month. With all this excitement *don't* forget that you have plants that need almost daily attention. Watering and combating diseases or pests are *musts*.

Potting On

1. If a plant is young and in good shape, it may simply be moved to a larger pot. (Warren Gray)

2. The healthy white root tips indicate that the roots are active and will make new growth when the plant is potted on. (Warren Gray)

3. The roots will indicate when the plant is ready to be potted on. When they curl around the bottom of the pot and before they get too tight, the plant should be moved into a pot large enough to allow 2 cm around the plant. Tease the roots apart a little before potting up. (Warren Gray)

Watering is stepped up during this month. It should be done in the early mornings of every second or third day, as some nights can still be quite cool. Wet foliage on plants caused by evening watering may bring down the temperature and check early spring growth. If flowering plants are on the benches, still use dust control methods for disease and pest control in the orchid house. Keep up with all potting work. Those who follow a fertilising programme should start with it this month. Often liquid fertilising is better than top dressing as there is less risk of clogging up open-growing mediums. Do not apply fertiliser to flowering plants. As all blooms are removed from a plant it should be prepared for its next twelve months, then placed in the growing area of the house where the fertilising is done.

Liquid Fertilising

Where a plant is required to make quick, sturdy growth a fertiliser is given as a stimulant. The idea is to make available certain elements that the plant can easily assimilate through its root system into the entire plant structure. Root-feeding liquid fertilisers should only be given to a plant while it is actively growing. The compost should be thoroughly moistened before applying them and should be kept that way for at least several days afterwards. To prevent clogging up of potting mixture, liquid fertilisers from animal sources should be vigorously stirred just before drawing off. Strain this through a sieve with a mesh of 3 mm. There are many 'homemade brews' that can be easily made up and satisfactorily used. A very simple one is as follows: Obtain an empty cask or drum, put into it one part fresh cow or fowl manure and add three parts water. Leave standing for several days to ferment. Stir occasionally. Draw off one part of strained liquid from this brew and add it to eight parts of water. Water lightly once a week with this during the growing season or for the time desired to get extra growth by a

The sensitive cells at the leaf tips of these plants have turned black because of damage from toxic substances which have been taken up by the plants. This may be due to excess fertiliser or to insufficient watering after applying fertiliser. (Warren Gray)

Cymbidium Flirtation 'Gold Dust'—a miniature type. (Don Jones)

stimulant. Before the bottom of the cask is reached, add a fresh lot of ingredients. This brings about a slight improvement in each mixture.

An excellent combined organic and inorganic liquid fertiliser may be made in the following manner: Use one part fresh cow manure, three parts water put down as the above brew. Have mixed dry in another container:

7 parts sulphate of ammonia
2 parts superphosphate
1 part sulphate of potash

Take 1.25 L of the strained liquid and 250 g of the dry fertiliser mixture and add both of these to 36 L of water. Apply lightly once weekly.

Should an entirely inorganic fertiliser be required, the following will give orchid plants all the necessary elements to grow to flowering stage and will keep them strong and healthy if growing conditions are correct:

2 level tablespoons ammonium phosphate
5 level tablespoons potassium nitrate
6 level tablespoons calcium nitrate
4 level tablespoons Epsom salts
115 L water

Water with this lightly once a week.

There are many liquid fertilisers on the market. These are quite beneficial if applied according to directions. The ratio of nitrogen, phosphorus and potash

(NPK ratio) is shown on all fertilisers sold in Australia. Many growers like to use different fertilisers at different times of the year. Slow-release fertilisers may be used in place of liquid feeding and trace elements may also be applied in a slow-release form. However liquid feeding is more accurate because strength and content can be changed during the growth cycle of the plant. If the mix is well drained, it is essential to keep the plants well watered to prevent a build up of soluble salts which may damage the roots.

Cymbidiums will take top dressing but this will break the mix down and clog it up if used too heavily or frequently. Two dressings during the active growing period seem quite satisfactory. A suitable dressing is 1 dessertspoon of pelleted fowl manure to each 200 mm pot. Alternatively, 1 dessertspoon of dried blood fertiliser or three-quarters of a teaspoon of the all-chemical liquid fertiliser in its dry state may be used. Remove the top 13 mm of compost, then spread the fertiliser over the surface, scratch it in a little, then cover with 13 mm of fresh orchid mix. Keep well watered after applying until all risk of burning is over. If growing only a few orchids for home decoration, do not fertilise heavily. Growing them in the mixture we recommend would be sufficient. Overdoing the fertilising of orchids can do much damage. You must 'feel' your way. When you are fertilising orchids heavily you must watch them very closely indeed. Fertilising, ventilation (air), water, warmth and light are all closely related. This means, that when heavy fertilising is being done all the other essentials must be adjusted to make the job really successful.

October

This should be another very active month for the cymbidium grower. Longer, warmer days and shorter, milder nights are starting all summer-growing orchids on a very active growing period, so we must ensure that all the plants are ready to obtain the maximum benefit from this. Keep up with all potting work. Get the plants growing vigorously. There are still plenty of blooms left on the cymbidium plants. As these start to lose their freshness, remove the spike carrying them and establish the plant for the next twelve months. Watering should be increasing to summer supply. This depends on the weather. It is risky to damp down after midday. Summer pests seem to appear one after the other.

Red Spider and Other Pests

Red spider is a sap-sucking mite that thrives in warm to hot, dry areas, mainly on the underside of the leaves of soft-leaved plants. It will take to many kinds of orchid leaves, including those of the cymbidium. It sucks the sap from the part attacked and leaves a small whitish patch. Red spider multiplies rapidly in favourable conditions and, if not checked, will number dozens in a very small area, each one sucking sap, each one leaving a whitish patch. Soon the whole area shows a greyish surface which is one of the first signs that red spider is attacking the leaves. They can be seen plainly by viewing them through a ×3 magnifying glass. They will quickly defoliate and kill a plant. This is often seen to happen to a patch of beans in the vegetable garden, if control measures are not being used during hot summer months. The leaves fall with the mites still on them. On windy days they are scattered over a wider area where they soon get a hold and in a matter of a day or two will spread right through large areas.

Many pots of cymbidiums have, besides the plant, a variety of weeds growing in them. One troublesome kind is the oxalis-clover family. Red spider will attack these weeds and when they have got all that they want from them they spread onto the leaves of the orchids. To keep the orchid house free of red spider, keep the house itself and its surroundings as free of weeds as possible.

Specific miticides have been developed to control this pest and obviously large collections of cymbidiums will have to be closely monitored and spraying undertaken if circumstances require. However, the ability of the insect to quickly build up a resistance to new miticides means that they have to become stronger, and, as a consequence, riskier to use, year by year.

A significant part of the control is now undertaken by the use of predator insects. Colonies of predator mites are introduced and encouraged to build up with the result that the need for spraying, as a control, is significantly reduced, or even eliminated, if conditions are suitable.

With a small collection, spraying should never become necessary if a few simple procedures are undertaken. Red spider mites like dry spots. Plants grown in tucked away corners of glasshouses where there is little air movement and generally dry, stagnant conditions will have the ideal home for them. Therefore try to ensure that the opposite applies.

The mites are usually to be found underneath the leaves, so when watering try to ensure that the water reaches this part of the plant and generally try to keep the humidity up in the shadehouse, particularly on days when dry westerly winds are prevailing. If you have a few rose bushes or are growing some beans in the vegetable garden, have a look under their leaves. If you find the mites there (and they seem to prefer them to cymbidiums) watch for their appearance on your orchids. It must be stressed that from the onset of warm weather every effort must be made to stop them getting a firm hold. They can be hard to see, but can be detected by running a finger or thumb up the leaf. If red spider is present, a grittiness will be felt.

Scale

These may not always be recognised as insects because the waxy coating secreted by the female looks like a small blister on the stem, leaf or bulb. They weaken the

Scale can be seen on this plant. Male scale, the white ones, are small and elongated. They form fluffy clumps. The females are larger and circular. They cause damage by sucking the sap. February is usually the worst month for scale infestation. (Warren Gray)

plant by sucking the sap and encourage the development of sooty moulds by secreting honeydew. Use soapy water to wash off as many as possible. White oil and Malathion will help control them.

Aphids
Because aphids are sap suckers they may affect the growth of plants and cause misshapen flowers. They may be removed by hand or hosed off the plants. Pyrethrum sprays intended for use in the garden are quite effective but will need to be repeated as eggs continue to hatch.

Thrips
Thrips will show up in patches. They are easily discerned as they can be readily seen with the naked eye. In their early stage of life, when they do most damage, they are wingless, sucking, yellow or black, soft-bodied insects, up to 1.5 mm long, that cluster on any tender parts of the plants. In the case of cymbidiums, the buds, blooms and the tops of spikes are most likely to be attacked. Because thrips attack in such numbers, they will quickly suck all sap from the top end of a spike showing buds and reduce it to a withered, disfigured ruin. Many insecticides such as Thiodan, Malathion and pyrethrum-based sprays are effective against them.

Mealy-bugs
Because these soft-bodied insects are covered with a white mealy substance and shelter in such places as leaf axils and around the base of stems and leaves as well as in the compost, they are often hard to detect before they have caused a good deal of damage. They are difficult to control. Malathion may be successful. There are a number of chemicals available to control insect pests, but because products are entering and leaving the market constantly, New South Wales Agriculture

Cymbidium Yowie Flame 'Heather'. (Don Jones)

and Fisheries recommends that the label be checked to see that it is registered for both the particular pest and for use on ornamentals.

Be sure to exercise extreme care in the use of all insecticides and fungicides. Their dangers must be recognised and measures taken accordingly. Remember that keeping plants healthy and surroundings clean is an important step towards preventing insect attacks.

November

The flower crop is over for another season. The few blooms that remain on a plant should be removed if it needs dividing as this job must soon be finished off. Once a new growth's leaves start to 'fan out' it is getting too late to divide that plant. It should be left until autumn. Keep the plants moist all the time by watering them every second or third day if it appears necessary; damp down on the other days.

Keeping diseases and pests in check should now become a priority. Apply liquid fertiliser now if extra growth is sought.

The care of the plants during the next few months will determine next season's crop of blooms.

How to Get Many Good Blooms

The main purpose of growing orchids is for the blooms they produce. It so often happens that these are not numerous enough. If a lead on an adult cymbidium has all its leaves and is strong and mature, by spiking season (January–February) it should produce one or more flower spikes. The embryo for the future spike on such a lead is now at a stage where it can be encouraged to develop.

Up until now the emphasis has been on strengthening the plants and bringing them to maturity by providing the best possible growing conditions, such as a well-balanced potting mix, correct use of fertilisers, dividing or reconditioning at least every two years and positioning plants to receive broken sunlight from early morning to late evening. From now until the spikes appear, many blooms are lost through incorrect shading. Both overexposure to sun or too much shade will prevent successful flowering. Take care not to lose your eagerly anticipated blooms by your treatment of the plants during the spiking season. The correct amount of light is crucial.

Some growers greatly increase shade at this time to produce lush growth. Indeed, plants growing in deep shade appear strong, as they have long, rich green leaves and large bulbs, but usually they will not flower because they lack sufficient sunlight. Their older bulbs defoliate early. They should never be given nitrogen fertilisers. Conversely, cymbidiums grown in full sunlight will usually grow weaker every year. Although the sun will not burn them if the moisture content of the soil is properly maintained, they will become stunted, with yellowish leaves and small bulbs that lose their leaves and turn into back-bulbs early. Eventually they are too weak to flower. Regular applications of liquid leaf-feeding nitrogen fertilisers will help these plants greatly. Also the roots of plants growing in direct sunlight will be damaged and this will weaken the plant below flowering strength unless the pot has been protected by a low sunbreak from becoming too hot and dry.

One can experiment by gradually moving a plant year by year from full sunlight to gradually deepening shade in order to find the position where the quality and quantity of blooms is as desired. Fortunately much experimenting is not necessary for the home grower. In areas where the temperature range is from 3 to 31°C (and only occasionally below or above), 66 per cent of direct sunlight shining onto the plants through 38 mm slats or commercially prepared shade-cloth seems a happy medium which keeps the plants strong and healthy. They will hold their leaves for several years and give plenty of strong spikes and good blooms. If a new growth is not mature at spiking time, a flower should be obtained from that growth as a leading bulb the following year. Sometimes a back-bulb is seen to produce a weakling spike. This is proof that the spike was 'lost' at the time when it should have appeared as a top-grade one. This is usually caused by overshading or conditions which are too cool in early spring.

Of the five essential factors (air, light, warmth, moisture and food) for growing plants from seedling stages to flowering and producing seed, the first two are very important and are free of costs, but in many instances they are the ones of which plants are most deprived in the orchid house. The surest way of obtaining many good blooms is by strengthening the plants, attending to them regularly and correctly and by giving them good measure of both air and filtered sunlight.

December

December is usually hot and dry and includes many holidays. During the month careful attention must be given to the watering of all plants. You will find that they will dry out quickly and extensive damage can be done in a few days if this dryness is allowed to last. So ... WATER REGULARLY.

Humidity can be high in the orchid house. This will start fungus diseases growing. They can cause damage which is not at the time readily discernible. The damage caused by fungi does not always become apparent immediately, sometimes not until several months later. In addition, summer pests multiply rapidly during this period and a few days' neglect of the orchid house may result in these pests taking charge and causing untold damage. So ... CHECK REGULARLY FOR PESTS AND FUNGUS GROWTH.

Holiday Time

A seasonal problem that strikes many orchid growers is: 'How are my plants going to fare while I am away from them for a fortnight's holiday?' In the August notes we explained how to retain moisture for three or four days at a time when plants are growing in very dry areas. By the use of similar methods, plants growing in quite small pots need not suffer through lack of moisture during your absence. Besides following the August recommendations it is advisable to pack the pots close together. Should they be exposed in a very open house, run planks, several layers of hessian or pieces of pliable plastic sheeting, rim high, close to the pots around the outside of them. This is to prevent side evaporation. Fill all crevices between the pots with wet material such as tan bark, orchid mix or waste newspaper. When all is set up, saturate the plants and surroundings with water just before leaving them. Wait until the top surface water has drained off then finish the holiday preparation by using a disease and pest preventive spray on the plants and all around their area. The pots are virtually buried to their rims in a wet, moisture-retaining bed where under normal conditions they should be quite all right for up to two or three weeks at a time.

Cymbidiums Outside the Temperate Climate Zone

Some folk living outside the temperate regions may wish to grow and flower cymbidiums but find it difficult to create an ideal climate condition for their plants to respond. It will assist these folk greatly and reduce their flowering problems considerably if they select plants which include hybrids with a strong lineage of a species whose natural habitat is a similar climate to theirs. There are species used in hybridising our modern hybrid cymbidiums that are found well outside the temperate zone regions, in either warmer or cooler climates.

Some species used in early hybridising are as follows:

Name	Origin	Climate
Cymbidium l'ansonii	Burma	Temperate
Cymbidium eburneum	Burma	Temperate
Cymbidium lowianum	Burma	Temperate
Cymbidium tracyanum	Burma	Temperate
Cymbidium insigne	Vietnam	Warmer
Cymbidium erythrostylum	Vietnam	Warmer
Cymbidium giganteum	Nepal	Cooler
Cymbidium grandiflorum	Nepal	Cooler

Warmer

In hot climates the very hot midday sun should be kept almost off the plants by housing them under a low and heavily shaded roof so built that it allows the early morning (to 9.30 a.m.) and late evening (after 5.00 p.m.) sun to shine right on to them. The benches should be high so that plenty of below-bench air-flow is available to the plants. The floor should be covered with wood shavings, blue metal, gravel or some such 'clean' litter which will hold moisture. The plants should be grown in a very open mix. Remove the fine particles from semi-terrestrial mix with a 6 mm mesh sieve. Use only the coarse mix. Repot with new mix every year. Do not fertilise heavily. Water or damp down frequently.

Cooler

Although the range is reduced in the selection of these plants there is quite a pleasing variety to be had. Plants being grown in cool areas must be housed differently during summer and winter. During the warmer summer months they should have sun to a degree where slightly stunted growth is apparent. During winter they must be protected from any really heavy frost and from being kept wet and cold with long winter rains. They would do best under a glass shelter or in a glasshouse. Another good winter site for growing a few plants would be at the back of a wide verandah facing north.

An addition of up to 15 per cent rich sandy loam in the growing mix keeps it warmer. This should greatly improve their chances of flowering normally. Watering should keep them just damp during winter months but get back to normal watering during the warmer, growing period.

Follow the monthly notes for general treatment of the plants growing in both warmer and cooler places.

3. *Paphiopedilum*

Usually it is not long before a keen orchid enthusiast acquires a few paphiopedilum plants. They have many advantages which make them desirable for a grower of a few orchids of mixed genera around the home. They require less light than many other types of orchids. A good position is one which receives little or no direct sun but good light. A closed-in verandah may be suitable. They make excellent house plants. Among paphiopedilums are found many with unusual shapes and colourings in

Paphiopedilum villosum 'Len-ray' CC/NSW—an easily grown slipper species from India and Nepal. (OSNSW)

Paphiopedilum Pathfinder Heritage 'Dundas' HCC/NSW. Slipper flowers are very rewarding. They last for months. (OSNSW)

Paphiopedilum Captain Cook 'Jon' HCC/NSW—a fine show-bench slipper.

Paphiopedilum (Challow × J. E. Walker) 'Northville' HCC/NSW. Top quality slipper orchids are easily grown and are very rewarding. (OSNSW)

almost every shade imaginable. The majority of them have a set flowering season once each year, the most attractive display of blooms occurring in mid-winter. This fact, of course, makes them desirable in any collection, as they provide blooms at a time when very little else is flowering. The blooms are very long lasting.

Paphiopedilum plants are practically disease free and very few pests attack them. With ordinary care in cultivation, and precautions against disease and pests, they can be easily flowered and kept clean and healthy.

Among the several essentials that define a plant as an orchid is the fact that its flowers have three sepals, three petals and one column (formed by the stamens and pistil being joined together). With paphiopedilum blooms there are usually only two sepals, the two ventral (lower) sepals being joined together. Occasionally they do not join. One petal usually departs from the pattern of the other two. This one is called the labellum. The paphiopedilum labellum resembles the front portion of a lady's slipper. Paphiopedilums are often referred to as 'lady's slipper' orchids for this reason.

These notes are written mainly for plants belonging to species of the genera that come from a region of South-East Asia (where there is a wide range of temperature) or for hybrids bred from these. They will be mainly those with broad, green leaves. As far as growing conditions are concerned they are very adaptable plants. The majority of them can be grown quite successfully in unheated glasshouses in the milder areas around Sydney. However, they do require slightly warmer growing conditions than do cymbidiums and their growing requirements are a little more exact.

Notes indicating any extra attention that they require are included in these pages. Some paphiopedilums must have a temperature of not less than 15°C. One easy general way of telling if a certain plant belongs to this warmer growing group is by a permanent, natural mottling of the leaves of that plant. There are exceptions however. There are some mottled leaf types which will grow 'cool', just as there are many green leaf types that require warmth.

January

During the hot, glary summer days, plants should be rather heavily shaded, especially those growing in glasshouses. Paphiopedilums are not gross feeders. If they are grown in the medium we recommend for them and repotted into fresh mixture each year there is no need to give them any extra fertiliser; however, there is no harm in using some sparingly. Maintain as much humidity as possible by watering the plants or damping down their house every day during normal weather. The first buds of the winter-flowering plants are now just starting to move. Bud rot often occurs at this stage. The main causes are:

1. the concentration of salts in and around the hearts of the plants where the buds are situated—so if using chemical sprays do not allow a heavy run off; or
2. a sudden drop in temperature when the plants have been watered in the evening. Always have an eye on the weather. Check, if available, the latest weather reports and be influenced by them when thinking of watering late in the evenings.

Any summer-flowering plants with blooms on now should be kept cool, moist and shaded to make these blooms last their full span.

February

During this month, as for January, the plants should be kept reasonably cool and moist but do not place them in a draught for coolness, nor let the pots become permanently wet while keeping the moisture up to the plants.

There is a troublesome pest that often appears among the paphiopedilums at about this time of the year. It is a soft, light brown scale. It usually shows itself first in corners where the light is strong and the air dry and warm. This damaging pest attaches itself mostly on the underside of the older leaves. Should it become established before being discovered, remove all old yellowing leaves and burn or bury them. Make up a solution of an insecticide and white oil to spray the affected plants and ensure a thorough spray coverage on the underside of the leaves. Where sheaths persistently hold water, this water should be removed or bud rot may occur. A strong puff of air will often blow it away. In some instances the plant may have to be turned almost upside down for a short while to remove it. In isolated, stubborn cases the water may have to be mopped out with a piece of blotting paper.

The more persistently the water stays around about a young developing bud the greater is the risk of getting bud rot. When watering flowering paphiopedilum plants keep water out of the pouch. Should any lodge there it must be removed or it will cause the bottom of the pouch to rot away with only a few waterings.

March

With the approach of shorter days and longer, cooler nights during this month, cultivation is considerably changed in the paphiopedilum house. Keep the plants' growing medium moist but avoid overhead watering on cloudy or cool days. Light is increased. Stake up all flower scapes as soon as possible. This will prevent misplaced blooms later on in the season. Use a straight piece of no. 10, or thinner, wire for the stake. Allow it to be long enough so that when in place it is level with the bloom when the scape is fully grown. Tie firmly around the stake and loosely around the scape at intervals of every 5–8 cm.

April

Work among the paphiopedilums should be much the same as during the last month. Those who are growing plants of the type preferring greater warmth should strive to maintain a temperature of not less than 16°C. The broad, green-leaved hybrids should be grown in a house with a temperature of not less than 10°C, for good results.

Watering is largely dependent upon the weather conditions, where the plants are being housed and the condition of the growing mixture. Watering in a heated house must be much greater than for plants growing in a cool one, while for those growing in two-year-old mixture, water is reduced. On cloudy or cool days watering must be reduced to the minimum. Any plants growing in a house heated to a minimum of 16°C should be watered daily. Those growing under cool, airy shelters should be watered every third or fourth day, while those growing in two-year-old, broken-down mixture must be watered in such a way that the mixture almost dries out after each watering.

After a general rain that thoroughly saturates the plants and their surroundings, as in the case of plants growing in a shadehouse, plants should be left at least five or six days before the first watering.

May–July

Watering is further reduced during these months. Eliminate completely overhead watering. If a plant in a shadehouse has an advanced bud, place that plant under a shelter if the weather should be at all adverse. Glasshouses with paphiopedilums growing in them should have all vents opened early in the mornings on sunny, mild days. See to it that they are closed during the early evening to preserve warmth.

Paphiopedilum tonsum 'Splendens' HCC/NSW. This Indonesian species is a warm grower. Some heat during winter in the southern States is necessary. (OSNSW)

Paphiopedilum World Spa 'Moonshine' HCC/NSW. Seedlings with potential to give flowers such as this are available from your favourite orchid nursery. (OSNSW)

This group of six paphiopedilums received a Silver Medal at an Orchid Society of NSW winter show. (OSNSW)

Paphiopedilum Gael 'Camira' AM/NSW—a fine maudiae type slipper. (OSNSW)

Group any flowering plants together in a conspicuous, cool, airy position to make a display of them for yourself, your family and your orchid-loving friends. From quite a small collection such a show can be kept going for quite long periods. Continue tying up the flower scapes. If these are kept upright the 'slipper' is usually presented pleasingly. Many slipper blooms are spoiled by letting the flower scape flop over horizontally until the bud opens and the flower becomes 'set' before straightening it up. If this is done the bloom will not be directly visible and the slipper will project out and up too prominently in front of the bloom.

Other defects that often spoil slipper blooms, and which can be corrected just as the bloom opens, are the revoluting of the dorsal sepal and the reflecting of the ventral sepal. An easy and effective way to correct either or both of these would be to make a soft 'bed' at the back of the bloom requiring correction. Making such a bed and holding it 'permanently' in position may be done by taking a piece of no. 10, or thinner, wire. Bend it around at about the middle, making a deep 'U' about 5 cm wide. Push the ends of the wire into the growing medium at the back of the bloom, with the bend about level with the top and about a centimetre from the back of the dorsal sepal. Pack up to the back of parts needing correction with pieces of soft, crushed tissue paper or pads of cotton wool, so placed that they hold the parts of the bloom, especially the sepals, where desired. After several days, when the bloom is 'set', the packing may be removed, after which the bloom will retain the desired shape. The sepals and petals of a good paphiopedilum bloom should be saucer shaped, neither flat nor cupped. The 'pouch' and ventral sepal should lie close together.

Prepare a batch of potting medium in July for use next month when it will be required.

An excellent potting medium for paphiopedilums is obtained as follows: remove the sand and fine dust from a semi-terrestrial orchid-growing medium and from fine pine bark with a 6 mm sieve. Mix equal parts of the two coarse materials.

August

A general spring, plant-growth movement will be noticeable from now on. The all important task now, in the paphiopedilum house, is to finish the repotting as quickly as possible. Start with those plants whose flowers are finished or those that missed out on flowering. Assemble the repotted plants in one area and lessen the bench area of the remainder. Always keep the groups (repotted and otherwise) separated. This will ensure that no plants are missed; also, the two groups may need slightly different watering.

Repotting is definitely an annual task with this genus unless the plants are grown in some of the especially long-lasting materials that are available in certain areas. Where timberyard wood shavings, pine bark and leaf-mould make up the bulk of the potting medium it is absolutely essential to repot annually. The task can be made a very easy and pleasant one, and, if a little extra care is given to the plants, it will also be very successful.

Right at the start there should be available plenty of seasoned potting medium and a good, hip-high potting bench to work on. It may be desirable to divide some of the plants. The actual breaking up of a paphiopedilum plant is not difficult and the plants re-establish themselves quickly after the operation. Paphiopedilum plants have no pseudobulbs as do so many of our other cultivated orchids. A short, jointed rhizome should send up, from the last season's growth, one or more new growths at about the same time each season. The flowers are produced from the centre of these new growths, as they mature, if the plant is ready to flower. As the growth ages, it gradually loses its leaves, so that after three or four years it is leafless and often dead, or nearly so. The rhizome under these old leafless growths (stumps) will also be about finished. If the rhizome has not been cut previously, as with back-cutting, it will break apart easily now.

Check a new plant for weak or damaged roots, removing any that may be found. If the new plant has an abundance of strong, healthy roots, remove some of the older ones and perhaps shorten others. This will encourage new roots to start on the new growths. At repotting time plants separate naturally, forming new ones. These new plants could be potted up singly. A weak plant would go into a 100 mm pot; a strong one into a 150 or 170 mm one.

Terracotta pots are lightly crocked, but be sure that at least one well-placed crock is used over a large drainage hole, with a few others so placed as to prevent the coarse medium from escaping. We expect the drainage to be in the potting mixture not the crocks. No crocking is necessary if using plastic pots. However, ensure that the drainage holes are such that they will be effective.

September–December

During these months the weather gradually warms up until by December very hot periods may be experienced. All potting should be finished and the plants well-established before these hot spells. Our experience shows that early spring is the most satisfactory time for potting. During the late spring and early summer, shade should be increased, until by the end of the year maximum shading is provided. This should remain until the cooler autumn weather sets in.

Throughout these months fresh air should be plentiful and, if the plants have been recently potted into the growing medium we recommend, they should be watered daily in normal weather. Keep an eye out for fungus diseases and insect pests and deal with them straight away.

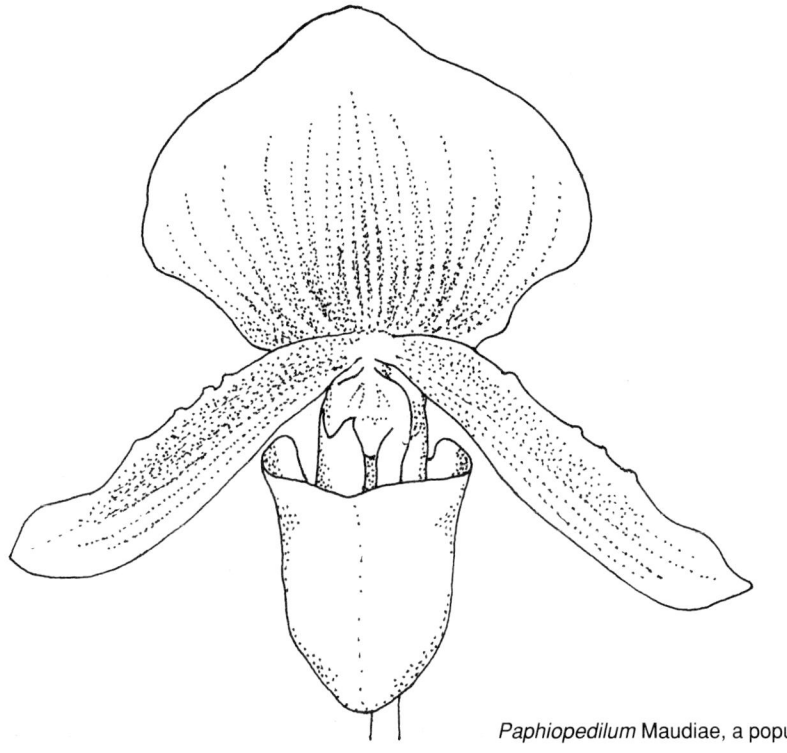

Paphiopedilum Maudiae, a popular slipper orchid.

4. Australian Natives

This is a very wide group of plants containing a wide range of genera and a wide range of types. They can be found growing on trees, on rocks, on the ground and in the ground.

The ground dwellers (terrestrials) are a very important and widely grown section of Australian native orchids. However, they tend to be grown by specialists and, in particular, growers who have a close association with one or more of the Australasian Native Orchid Society (ANOS) groups. Anyone who is interested in terrestrials is advised to seek membership of one of these groups. The main body can be contacted at PO Box 106-C, Clarence Street, Sydney NSW 2000.

This chapter will accordingly concentrate on what are loosely called the epiphytes, and specifically *Dendrobium* and *Sarcochilus*, which form the backbone of collections. There are some genera outside of these two that are to be found at orchid meetings and shows. An example is *Cymbidium* of which Australia has three species (*C. suave*, *C. madidum* and *C. canaliculatum*) and there are hybrids arising therefrom. In very general terms the requirements as outlined under the chapter on cymbidiums can be followed. *C. madidum* in fact will thrive under such culture. *C. suave* and *C. canaliculatum* do require a little more care in the area of watering.

Cymbidium suave grows in trees or tree stumps and the roots travel quite a distance through the soft internal sections thereof. They can travel up to 6 m. They resent disturbance, so should be placed in a mix which can be expected to last for a few years. Watering, too, must be adapted to these requirements. *C. canaliculatum* is found growing in areas where humidity is generally lower than that applying in coastal climates. Growers usually have their plants in a much coarser mix containing more bark than that recommended for cymbidiums generally. They are kept apart from the other cymbidiums so they can be given individual treatment. Suffice to say that if they, or hybrids with this species as one of the parents, are included with the general collection of cymbidiums, the chance of having them succumb to one of the fungus or bacterial diseases will be high.

The growing of Australian native orchid species is as popular now as it was when the first edition of this book was published. The environment and conservation are such topical subjects that this interest can only increase as the years go by. Habitats of many of the Australian orchid species have disappeared or have significantly decreased over the years, so species which once were abundant are now scarce in nature.

Efforts have been made by many growers to take the pressure off the remaining wild populations by raising in nurseries quantities of them for general release. In undertaking these activities the growers select, for breeding, the best available clones of the species so that the plants released can be expected to give flowers of much higher quality than can be found in the wild. Again this helps the wild populations. There has also been wide and varied work done by hybridists over the past twenty-five years with many of the current hybrids being very floriferous and attractive. These hybrids have extended the previous rather narrow flowering season of the species. Ira Butler trophies are issued each year (named in honour of the pioneer of hybridising in this area) to winners of the Australian native orchid hybrid classes at shows and this has also ensured a strong interest in developing them even further.

In the genus *Dendrobium*, *D.* Bardo Rose, *D.* Ellen, *D.* Delicatum, *D.* Hilda Poxon are all very popular hybrids and will be seen in virtually all shows where Australian

Sarcochilus falcatus 'Miriam Ann' HCC/NSW—a very popular Australian epiphyte known as the orange blossom orchid. (OSNSW)

native orchids participate. In the genus *Sarcochilus*, *S.* Fitzhart and *S.* Melba remain popular many years after the first flowerings were seen and in fact are being remade each year to cater for the significant demand.

Shade of around 50 per cent will be quite suitable for the dendrobiums, both species and hybrids, year round, although they like up to 30 per cent shade during the cooler months. The extra light is thought to assist with flower production. *Sarcochilus*, as a general rule, like more shade (70 per cent on average).

Air circulation is a vital factor in good, healthy growth, a gentle breeze through the plants being the optimum. Try to avoid stale, stagnant conditions. The plants will not like them and, in any event, they will encourage pests and diseases—natives are as open to attack as any other orchid. If any problem is noted, it should be dealt with in accordance with the recommendations outlined in the special sections on pests and diseases on pages 22–7, 31, 36 and 48–51.

There is, however, one particularly nasty pest that loves Australian native dendrobiums. It is the dendrobium beetle, which has been their natural predator over many centuries. The damage done by the actual insect is very significant and is certainly very noticeable in a collection; however, it is the larvae which are the real problem. These larvae actually find their way into the pseudobulbs of the plants and during the course of their development they create havoc, virtually destroying them and, as a consequence, preventing flowering from that growth.

Plants can be killed through their efforts. It helps if a daily inspection is undertaken to get early warning of their presence. Shredded leaves are a tell-tale sign. The beetles can most often be found on the flowers and should be caught and destroyed when seen. If disturbed, they allow themselves to drop to the surface of the pot or even to the ground where they will not move for several minutes. When located, therefore, the first step is to place a hand immediately under them where hopefully they will then fall. Destroy them immediately. Some growers actually grow plants of *Nepenthes* species (pitcher plants) in and around their shadehouse to alert them to the presence of the beetles. The beetles are attracted to these carnivorous plants and the pitchers quickly show evidence thereof.

As far as growing mix is concerned, both *Dendrobium* and *Sarcochilus* species and hybrids are fairly easygoing. A small- to medium-sized bark mix, with the addition of some pea-sized river gravel, suits them well, however, other ingredients can be added providing they do not affect the aeration qualities.

Watering follows the general requirements for most orchids, that is, plenty of water and moisture and humidity when in active growth, tapering off to once every couple of weeks when the plants are dormant. Fertilising follows this same general trend. They respond very well to feeding at a rate of say half to three-quarters the strength applied to cymbidiums.

There is no need to repot every year as is recommended for many genera. Providing the mix remains open, they will continue to grow happily for three to four years. Generally, repotting is only necessary when the plants outgrow their pots or when there is some obvious sign of distress.

January–March

Watering, shading and feeding are the important factors over this period. Dendrobiums under 50 per cent shade will be showing a yellowing of the leaves, however this will not do them any harm. In nature, colonies of *Dendrobium kingianum* and *D. speciosum* are often found on exposed rock faces where they have no protection from the full summer sun. There is therefore no need to treat them as delicate plants. It is necessary, though, to ensure that the root area is kept moist. In the wild, plants on exposed rock faces will have roots well into crevices and cracks in the rocks from whence moisture will be drawn. Plants in pots do not have this option, so regular watering is essential.

Keep a close watch for dendrobium beetles which will be very active.

Sarcochilus species and their hybrids need more care during these hot summer months. As mentioned, these notes do not cover the true epiphytes *(S. falcatus, S. hillii;* etc.) but the species *S. hartmannii, S. fitzgeraldii* and *S. ceciliae* and hybrids derived from them. These three species are, as a general rule, found in more shady and sheltered areas, where they do not suffer from the extremes possible in summer. There are exceptions of course, however it is soon obvious that they do not like the summers experienced at low elevations and close to the sea, where humidity is generally higher than slightly inland. They almost become dormant at this time of the year and it is quite apparent that they welcome the arrival of autumn and the first chill of the season.

April–May

These are months of quite a deal of activity. The dendrobiums will be tapering off their growth preparatory to initiation of flowers. Days are shorter and nights cooler, so, if possible, more light can be given. Plants must still be kept moist, but watering is effectively reduced. Fertilising can be reduced as well.

Sarcochilus species are a different matter though, and it is now a good time to undertake some activities not normally associated with the pre-winter orchid culture. Sarcochilus plants have the habit, in culture at least, of producing extensive root growth in autumn, maybe as a sign of relief that the hot weather is finished. It is accordingly a good time to repot them, if necessary, into fresh mix. The new root system will quickly establish the plant and it will go into winter with a strong and happy disposition. After repotting, wait for the new root growth before commencing heavy watering. All the plants, whether recently repotted or not, should still be kept moist.

June–July

Watering is now reduced to such an extent that the grower can virtually rely on normal precipitation (rain and dew) to provide the necessary moisture. The arrival of dry westerly winds will, however, make it necessary for some water to be applied. They must not dry out as this will have a detrimental effect on their flowering.

Clean plants up ready for flowering, that is, remove old leaves and inflorescences and generally tidy up the whole collection. Keep a watch out for pests. Caterpillars will make short work of the emerging inflorescences if there are any left after the snails and slugs have had their meals. Scale insects could also be evident. Treat as recommended on pages 49–50.

August–September

These are the months which Australian native orchid growers await with high expectations. The dendrobiums should now be in flower or well on their way to flowering. This is when the year's efforts give their reward. Apart from endeavouring to avoid any damage to the flowers and the inflorescences there is little in the way of hard work to be undertaken.

This is the flush season for the dendrobiums, so it is a good time to get around the shows to see what the hybridists have achieved over recent years.

Make a note of crosses or clones for your 'want' list when you go to your local

Dendrobium canaliculatum 'Lloyd' CC/NSW. A very popular Australian species which does best in the warmer northern areas. (OSNSW)

Dendrobium speciosum var. *curvicaule* 'Bicentennial' HCC/NSW. A fine clone of this northern Queensland variety. (OSNSW)

Dendrobium speciosum var. *hillii* 'Gum Nut' CC/NSW. The only disadvantage with the Australian rock lily, or king orchid, is that it is difficult to transport plants to meetings and shows. (OSNSW)

Dendrobium Bardo Rose CC/NSW—the result of crossing two Australian native orchids: *Dendrobium kingianum* and *Dendrobium falcorostrum*. (OSNSW)

orchid nursery. So many hybrids have been registered over recent years that it becomes very difficult for all but the ardent orchid grower to keep track of the names. If, at a show, you see a plant of, say, a *D. Essie Banks*, make a note of the name. When you go to the orchid nursery ask if the proprietor has any seedlings of this cross. You may find he has many of them sitting on the benches but they are listed as *D. Hilda Poxon* × *D. speciosum* (the parents of *D. Essie Banks*). Unless you ask you may never know that the plant you want is sitting right in front of you.

Sarcochilus species will be showing their inflorescences preparatory to their October flush. Keep a watch on them to ensure that they are not removed during the night by snails or slugs or their ilk.

October

Dendrobiums have now virtually finished their season so they can be broken up or repotted if necessary.

We are now entering the season when dendrobium beetles start their destructive activities. Watch closely for any sign of them. Remember the more beetles you can kill, the less larvae there will be to destroy the bulbs as they form during the growing season.

Sarcochilus species and hybrids will now be out in their full glory. Make a point of visiting some of the late shows to catch a glimpse of this delightful and beautiful group of plants. This month can be one of changing weather conditions and is traditionally a time for periods of wet weather. Your flowering plants should be under cover if possible so as to avoid the marking of the flowers which will be caused by exposure to rain. If you have aspirations to do some breeding with sarcochilus orchids now is the ideal time. However, follow one simple basic rule: Only breed with the best clones available. There is an accepted principle that if you breed with rubbish you will only get rubbish. Of course this does not always apply, however it is a good maxim to follow.

November–December

Australian native orchids will now be well into their active growth phase and should have many new bulbs on their way, in various stages of development.

Watering and feeding should now be maintained at the maximum level necessary to ensure the plants are never allowed to dry out. Try to time your watering so as to prevent the plants from actually being wet on very hot days. Because of their structure many of the new growths will hold water in their developing leaves. If water is so present on hot days, it will be heated and the growth will be partially 'cooked'. This is not appreciated by the plant and it will quickly show its displeasure.

Shading of sarcochilus is now very important. If you removed some of the shade to give added light for the winter months, it must be replaced now. November in particular can have several very hot and dry days. These are decidedly not to the liking of sarcochilus, so everything must be done to have conditions as pleasant as possible.

It is too late now to break up or repot your plants, unless there is some very pressing need. Hold them over until March if possible.

5. *Dendrobium*

These are popular plants with many orchid growers. If they are housed and cared for correctly they are easy to grow and flower. They grow over a wide area where climate differs greatly. Many of them like a position providing ample light and most require a definite rest period after their new growths are fully grown. They are true epiphytes and must be treated as such, that is, grown in small pots in a very open, firm growing medium. They are particularly free of diseases but there are two reasons why the flowers do not always develop as they should:

1. Young flower pedicels may turn into small aerial plantlets because of incorrect cultivation. The main cause of this is trying to flower a plant whose stems are not 'ripened', or suddenly giving the plant too much spring warmth and humidity when it starts developing its flower nodes.
2. The plant may experience bud-drop, usually caused by trying to grow the particular plant under conditions which are too cool or damp or where the air is too still or humid.

Snails, slugs and grubs attack dendrobiums at any time throughout the year. They attack not only the buds and flowers but also any roots they can reach, as well as young growths and leaves. Dendrobiums should be treated for diseases and pests and liquid fertilisers should be applied just as for other orchids growing in their neighbourhood. For housing and cultural notes we will divide them into two groups: softcane and hardcane.

Softcane Dendrobiums

These plants are made up mainly of the Indian *Dendrobium nobile*, together with its many varieties and hybrids. They grow well and flower freely in a shadehouse in a temperate zone climate. They need hot, humid summer conditions for growing their new stems to flowering size and strength, and cold winter conditions to ripen them to a flowering stage. The majority of them have whitish, rose-tipped, coloured flowers, though they may also be obtained in pure white, clear yellow and deep rose. They are very charming orchids. Some other attractive members of this diverse genus that are suitable subjects for growing in the same type of shadehouse as the above are as follows:

Name	Colour	Flowering time
Dendrobium aggregatum	Orange	Spring
Dendrobium chrysanthum	Yellow-orange	Autumn
Dendrobium chrysotoxum	Rich yellow	Summer
Dendrobium densiflorum	Orange-yellow	Spring
Dendrobium fimbriatum	Yellow, maroon blotch	Summer
Dendrobium griffithianum	Orange	Summer
Dendrobium pierardii	Rose-pink	Spring
Dendrobium thyrsiflorum	White, yellow centre	Spring

Many in this group do not form aerials as freely as do the species *Dendrobium nobile* and its varieties and hybrids, so are harder to propagate and obtain. They are more touchy in their growing requirements, especially they resent being grown in sodden, broken down mixture which is constantly wet. They are often slower growers, so take longer to fill a pot, with the result that often too much time is left before the changing of their growing medium. If their mix is too damp, the roots gradually die back until there is only a tuft of weak, stumpy ones around the base of the stems. Under these conditions the plants will soon die out. They can be grown and flowered successfully by keeping them in small pots, in a mixture which is kept sweet by being allowed to almost dry out occasionally and by being changed regularly (every second or third year). Their needs should be attended to as follows, according to their seasonal growing habits.

The cultural notes here are meant mainly for *Dendrobium nobile*, its varieties and hybrids, growing in a shadehouse in a temperate zone. They will also give a good indication of how to manage other plants of this group, as most of them need similar cultural treatment. Some may flower in different seasons of the year, so the flower nodes appear at different times.

Dendrobium Yukidaruma 'King' CC/NSW. Results like this can be achieved using basic culture aimed at satisfying the plant's specific needs. (OSNSW)

Dendrobium Lowana Red 'R. D. Hughes' HCC/NSW—an example of the so-called hardcane type dendrobiums. (OSNSW)

Dendrobium thyrsiflorum 'Iluka' CC/NSW—another easily grown Indian species which rewards its owner with a profusion of flowers in late spring. (OSNSW)

March

Try to stop growth without injuring the plants by ceasing the use of liquid fertiliser, easing up with watering and placing the plants in a cool position giving 90 per cent daylight where they will remain until spring. This is to harden off (ripen) the new stems and bring the plants to the flowering stage. The medium will last longer in the pots if the plants are housed under a shelter, out of rain, during the autumn and winter months, when very little water is required by these orchids. Water at intervals of once a fortnight or longer, according to the weather and the condition of the growing medium. Even for plants completely under shelter, watering once a fortnight is plenty, during their dormant period. Let the mixture dry right out occasionally. Just water enough to prevent damage to roots and shrivelling of stems.

June

During this month the flower nodes should be starting to develop on these orchids. They appear near the base of the leaves, near the top of each well-grown, mature, one- or two-year-old stem. The leaves grow alternately more than halfway down to the base and normally fall from two-year-old stems. These plants should develop and flower at about the same rate and time as do the blossoms on summer fruit trees (peaches, plums, etc.). Any attempt now to force the plants to flower earlier than normal may turn these incipient flower nodes into young plantlets (aerials). Just leave the plants where they are and water them sparingly.

August

During this month buds of many of the plants will break from their sheaths. Normally, watering is slightly increased when the buds appear. However, for controlled flowering, the treatment of plants is slightly different.

If early flowers are wanted, give the plants more warmth and keep it up to them day and night. With the extra warmth the plants must not be allowed to dry out at their roots. Humidity must not be allowed to drop below abut 75 per cent for long periods, or the flowers, when open, will be papery in substance; they will not have good colour nor will they keep well. Cause air movement to keep the plants in good condition and to prevent flower spotting.

For delayed flowering keep the plants even cooler, drier and more shaded. Keep them just sufficiently dormant not to injure them or their flower buds.

Flowering can be advanced or delayed by up to two weeks either way. Controlled flowering is mainly used to bring plants and flowers to their peak for entering into a show whose date is fixed and advertised well beforehand.

October

From this month onwards every provision should be made to ensure perfect growing conditions. Plants should be always moist, with a fresh warm and humid atmosphere. Weekly application of the organic and inorganic fertiliser (see page 47) should be given and light during the day should be about 50 per cent shade. Maintain these conditions until about the end of February, when a start should be made to harden off and ripen the new growths. When the flowers are almost open, the new active eyes will start to grow, though they are rather slow and weak at the beginning. As summer warmth begins to increase growth, the stems begin growing faster and stronger and will start to thicken near the top. This process will continue while the warmth and all the other good conditions last.

As autumn weather slows growth, the tops of the new growths become narrower. It is the plump section of the stem that produces the good flowers. The longer and plumper this section is, the better and more numerous will be the flowers. On small plants the stems should be staked and trained to remain upright. On specimen plants they should be spread evenly around the plant, with some upright, others arching and the remainder pendulous.

Repotting should be done soon after the flowering time when the new stems start sending out young root tips. This usually occurs when spring weather becomes fairly stable (Sydney, October). Plants are grown in medium-sized pots. Put a plant of three or four stems into a 100 or 125 mm pot. Choose a long-lasting growing medium. Strong-growing plants can be potted on repeatedly, each season, until large specimens are built up. Back-cutting can also be done at about this time. When doing this always leave at least three stems on the front section of the plant. When last season's aerials start sending up new growths, these aerials may then be removed from their parent stem and potted up singly in 75 mm pots.

Hardcane Dendrobiums

These are sometimes referred to as Cooktown orchids. Their natural habitat is along the far north coast of Queensland and its adjacent islands. Knowledge of the places of origin is a pointer to the requirements of this group of orchids. They will thrive only in tropical regions or in heated glasshouses in a temperate zone or cooler climate. To be grown well year after year and flowered successfully they need strong light, a day temperature of from 24 to 29°C and a night temperature that must not fall far below 13°C. Colder temperatures will cause a gradual decline in the plant's growing strength, as well as bud and flower drop, if they do flower. After several seasons in low temperatures the plants will surely die out.

When grown in their correct environment they are among the easiest of orchids to handle and their flowers are exceedingly lovely, being often up to 65 mm across and obtainable in shades varying from purple, through lavender and mauve to white. The hybrid flowers range up to 65–90 mm in diameter, some are even larger. They have a great variation in flower shape. *Dendrobium bigibbum* var. *phalaenopsis* has flat, full flowers, the petals being nearly as broad as they are long. The sepals are about one-third as broad as they are long. *D. stratiotes* has long, waved or twisted sepals; the petals are even longer, narrow, twisted and usually erect. The general appearance of the flowers gives this and a group of its hybrids the name of 'antelope orchids'. *D. discolor* has twisted and waved sepals and petals.

These species will cross-pollinate. This has been repeatedly done and many resulting hybrids have flowered. In shape the flowers are somewhat between the different parents. Plants of this group must be grown in a coarse, firm, always sweet medium, in small pots or on slabs of treefern fibre that is from 25 to 40 mm thick and large enough to give the roots good rambling space. A slab of fibre 230 × 100 × 40 mm would be ideal to mount a three- or four-stem plant to grow for several years. When grown in a temperate zone, the *bigibbum* type flowers mainly during the late autumn or early winter months. Many of the antelope type will flower at any time of the year. Often the same plant will flower twice in a year, and sometimes more frequently. All the flowers of this group are long lasting. Plants grow aerials occasionally. These are welcome as they make up quickly. If they are taken off their parent plant at potting time, potted out singly and cared for correctly they should flower as two year olds.

The cultural notes here for this group of plants are meant mainly for glasshouse growing plants in a temperate zone.

March

The correct method of watering these plants is the main concern at this time of the season. Be guided by the way they obtain their natural supplies. Although the temperature varies but little in their natural home there is a distinct wet and dry season. The new stems are grown during the wet. They flower during the dry when they rely mainly upon dew, at night or early morning, for their moisture requirement. Similarly keep the water up to the plants while growing, but reduce it considerably during the flowering period. At this time, water during the mornings and then only sparingly. Should cool nights be experienced, start using whatever heating arrangement is available.

Thin spikes can be observed starting to sprout from near the top of advanced, mature new stems and also old ones. Even three- and four-year-old stems will flower yearly if the plants are growing in ideal conditions. The plants near the glass may have to be lowered slightly, as upright spikes must not place the buds too near the glass. During cool nights and cloudy days keep the vents closed to preserve warmth. If humidity is high in the house it is wise to have a small fan running. This will help the plants maintain a hardy, healthy condition, also it will do much to prevent any bud- or flower-drop or spotting. During warm, sunny days have all vents fully open and keep them so for as long as possible to get a thorough change of air.

November

Try to get new growths away to an early start this month. If this can be managed, good stems should be produced before the shorter days and cooler nights stop their growth. Keep the plants high up in the glasshouse, right up to within a foot of the glass, as they thrive on the extra warmth and light there. Give the plants a daily soaking while they are actively growing but let them be dry by nightfall if the temperature is likely to drop below 18°C. Apply liquid fertiliser to the plants at least once a week. Dipping the pots into the liquid for about a minute is much better than just watering them with it.

Repotting should be attended to just as the new growths begin. If a strong plant is growing in a very small pot, smash the pot and repot the whole plant into a pot a size larger. Fill in the crevices with growing medium the same as when potting up a plant. Do not try to pull away pieces of the shattered pot. Back-cut wherever possible. If the plants are left to their own devices they often grow a single rhizome right across the pot. On the other hand softcane dendrobiums are more liberal in sending up growths. They often grow to dense clusters of stems by their own effort.

Dendrobium New Moon 'Cecil Park' CC/NSW. Modern breeding is aimed at achieving very floriferous plants. (OSNSW)

6. *Oncidium* Alliance

This is a very broad group covering many different, but closely related, genera. Several are so obscure and remote that they are seldom seen in collections; others are horticulturally very important and include some of the most impressive and desirable plants in a comprehensive collection. The main genera are *Oncidium, Odontoglossum, Miltoniopsis, Miltonia* and *Brassia*.

Oncidium

The genus *Oncidium* is perhaps, as the name implies, the most important one in the alliance. However, even within the *Oncidium* genus there is such a diversity of types as to make other than very general comments impossible. There are 'mule-eared' types, 'rat-tailed' types, 'equitant' types, as well as others that are not included in such loose headings. But by far the most important is the 'varicosum' type. These are the ones that fit fairly easily, both as far as type of flower and growth habit are concerned, with the species *Oncidium varicosum*. This species is the yellow 'dancing lady' orchid often seen at shows during the autumn. Varicosum types are ideal beginners' orchids. They have a definite growth/rest cycle and so long as this is generally observed, will reward the grower every year.

In sub-tropical and temperate areas (at least as far south as the New South Wales–Victorian border) they are shadehouse subjects year round, though preferably with some cover during the winter months, not for warmth, but to keep winter rains away from them. Many growers have naturalised them on trees in their gardens (frangipani and jacaranda are ideal) where they grow well, taking in their stride everything nature wishes to thrust upon them.

They can be grown in pots in a medium to large bark type mix, however they are happier when roots are allowed a free run, either on a tree or on a piece of treefern, hardwood, cedar or such. Just hang them up in the shadehouse under about 50 per cent shade, keep them well watered during the warm months, and they will grow very well. During this growth period, they will willingly accept whatever feeding is being delivered to the cymbidiums. Care will need to be taken on very hot days to ensure some moisture is available every day. Plants on slabs will dry out very quickly and although they have a moisture reserve in their bulbs, they must not be placed under stress.

In late summer the inflorescences will appear in the leaf axils preparatory to flowering in April or May. The green caterpillar known as the 'looper' considers the developing inflorescence as a delicacy not to be missed, so a very close watch will need to be maintained for this pest. Despite precautions, virtually every grower who has several plants will lose flowers in this way every year, the main reason being that it only takes such as short time for the damage to be done.

After flowering is finished, usually by the end of May or early June, remove the old inflorescences. The plants are now resting and they require virtually no attention until their next growth cycle starts, usually between the end of August and mid- to late September depending upon the local climatic conditions.

Because parts of eastern Australia receive winter rains, which are not well received by the resting plants, many growers place their plants under cover during the cold months. Temperatures can, and do, get down to slightly below freezing with no adverse effect on them and in fact they actually seem to benefit from the enforced rest with better growth the next year. They definitely do not respond to being forced to grow during the cold months, say by, for example, being kept in a heated glasshouse.

Repotting, or more correctly rehousing, need only be done as necessary. If they are grown on a slab of some kind they could be happy for years. Salt build-up or mix breakdown is not a problem so the only general limitation is the staying power of the host. If on cedar, they will only need attention when they outgrow it; if on a tree, there is effectively no limit.

Most orchid nurseries have stocks of seedlings of this type as they are very popular within the orchid-growing world. Hybridists have extended the flowering season dramatically and while autumn is their main season, it is now possible to have flowers in summer and spring.

Odontoglossum

The *Odontoglossum* genus, and two or three very closely related genera, are horticulturally very important. They are generally found in much higher elevations than the varicosum type oncidiums already referred to and, as a consequence, they have separate requirements. These place more demand on the abilities and resources of the grower. There has been some hybridising with *Oncidium* species and hybrids and the resultant plants are not too difficult.

Species and hybrids of Odontoglossum do not appreciate hot, humid summers which are far removed from the conditions they receive on their mountainside habitats in nature, where moist cool air is the norm, even in the high point of summer. Cold winters are not too much of a problem provided the plants are not expected to sit with wet feet on a cold frosty morning where the temperature does not start to rise until late in the morning. They are grown by most enthusiasts in glasshouses with summer cooling facilities and perhaps with some winter warmth. They are grown almost exclusively in pots, probably because they have been well domesticated over the past fifteen or so decades. They like a relatively fine mix which must, however, be well aerated as well as having some moisture-retaining ability.

Odontoglossums must be kept moist at all times. They never like to be dry. They respond excellently to feeding as evidenced by bulbs increasing in size each year. The only limit on the amount of feeding they will take is that if too much is given the bulbs may actually split as a consequence.

In nature they do not experience a high light intensity, probably due in part to the cloud cover usually associated with their habitats, so shading around 70 per cent, increasing during the hotter months, is required as a minimum.

Inflorescences can occur at virtually any time of the year. They come from the leaf exits and are as susceptible to the looper caterpillar as their oncidium cousins. There is therefore a need to watch for this pest. Otherwise they are very hardy plants, with mealy-bug possibly being next on the list as far as problems are concerned.

It is difficult to recommend a specific time for repotting or division. Mainly it is a case of each plant being taken on its respective merits. The time to repot is when the new growth is 100 mm or so high. This can be at any time of the year.

Seedlings of odontoglossums are carried by most orchid nurseries because of their popularity. They come in a range of colours and most have beautiful and unique markings.

Miltoniopsis

Previously known as 'pansy' type miltonias, these have to be one of the most rewarding genera available in the orchid world. The ratio of flower production to pot

Odontioda Murray River 'Golden Fire' AD/NSW. Hybridisers are bringing intense and interesting colours into the general *Odontoglossum* section. (OSNSW)

Alexanderara (*Maclellanara* Pagan Lovesong × *Odontioda* Janis Andrew) 'Starburst' HCC/NSW—a fine hybrid from the *Oncidium* Alliance. This clone won champion in its class at the 1988 Australian Orchid Conference Show. (OSNSW)

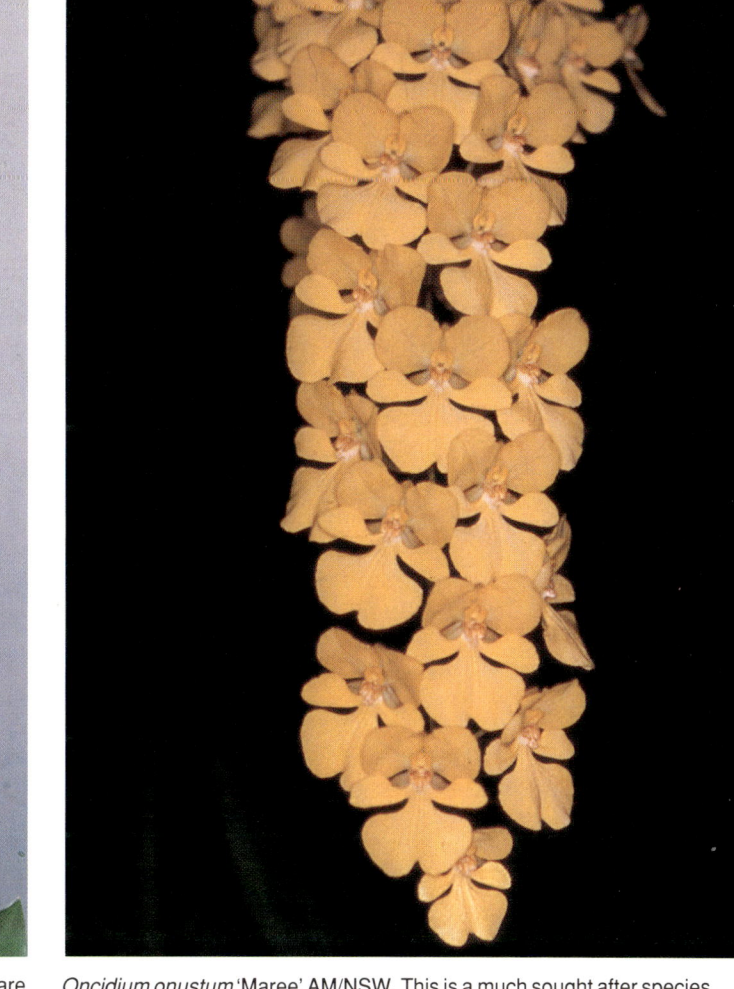

dontoglossum Pascoe Vale 'Camira' HCC/NSW. These hybrids are coming very popular in the southern States of Australia. Cool conditions t them well. (OSNSW)

Oncidium onustum 'Maree' AM/NSW. This is a much sought after species, sometimes thought of as being a little difficult to grow well. (OSNSW)

Oncidium (Golden Cloud × Shower of Gold) 'Amanda Jane' AM/NSW. The so-called varicosum type oncidiums grow very easily. They can be grown attached to host trees (frangipani is excellent) in and around the Sydney area. (OSNSW)

size is excellent. The only reason more are not grown is that they are even more specific in their needs than the odontoglossums. Not only do they need cooling in summer but also warmth in winter. They require a temperature range of 12–30°C, no warmer. They do not have any noticeable rest period, appearing to be in active growth year round.

They require more light than the odontoglossums and must be kept moist. This is a must. Drying out will have very adverse results as far as plant health is concerned. They love to be fed and will quickly respond thereto. A large plant, in its fine bark mix, will be quite happy in a pot up to a maximum of 125 mm. In fact scores of flowers can be achieved from such a pot size. Because they are grown in glasshouses where conditions are controlled, pests are usually not the problem they would be in an open shadehouse, nevertheless the usual precautions need to be taken.

Most orchid nurseries will have seedlings or can recommend a source. Because of their specific needs, nurseries will warn the potential buyer of these requirements.

Other Types

Included here are the true *Miltonia* (the warmer growing close relative of *Miltoniopsis*) and *Brassia*. Both of these are easily managed in the shadehouse under much the same conditions as for cymbidiums, maybe with more of a definite rest for the brassias in winter.

Extensive hybridisation has been done both within each genus and between the genera, so much so that the orchid hobbyist is offered a wide, appealing and unique range of types, colour, flowering seasons, etc. No matter what type of conditions he or she has (within reason of course) there will be plants that will fit neatly into the niche provided. With the restrictions on space being encountered by the community in general, and the orchid grower in particular, they are the obvious orchids of the future.

January–February

Varicosum type oncidiums will be growing strongly in the shadehouse now and the pseudobulbs will be filling out, preparatory to flowering. They love to be fed, so they may be fertilised every weekend. Ensure that they receive heavy waterings between fertilising sessions so as to prevent salt build-up. Towards the end of this period, inflorescences will start to emerge from the leaf axils. Watch out for snails, slugs and especially the green looper caterpillar. One bite at the end of the emerging inflorescence will mean no flowers during the autumn.

Odontoglossums need to be kept as cool as possible. Do not let them dry out at any time. They can be fertilised regularly, every week or ten days, however if they are under stress because of severe temperatures, concentrate on just keeping them as cool as possible. Feeding can be resumed when weather conditions are more conducive to growth.

On very hot days, if possible, damp down the floor of the shadehouse and wet the sides in an effort to provide some evaporative cooling. Specialist growers will have their plants in cooled glasshouses.

Miltoniopsis plants seem to be even more sensitive to the hot weather than the odontoglossums just mentioned. They must be kept cool but preferably with more light than for odontoglossums. Some sort of cooling is virtually essential for their continued growth during this period. They must not be allowed to dry out. There will be some signs of early inflorescences so the usual precautions need to be taken to ensure they are not lost to pests.

March–April

Odontoglossums and miltoniopsis plants require a virtual continuation of the January–February culture, that is, care must be taken to avoid heat stress and maintenance of the watering schedule and feeding is necessary if the weather conditions are such that the plants will be growing actively. Some odontoglossums will have inflorescences emerging so these need to be carefully nurtured. Some miltoniopsis plants will also be well on their way to flowering.

Varicosum type oncidiums are now at their peak flowering stage. Other than staking the inflorescences to ensure that they are not broken by wind or rain (they become very heavy when wet), it is really only a matter now of enjoying the flowers. The floral display produced by such relatively small pseudobulbs, is such that there is a significant drain on the strength of the plant if flowers are left on for too long. Some shrivelling of the pseudobulbs is natural, however too much means that the inflorescence should be removed in order to have a healthy plant going into winter.

May–August

Odontoglossums will now be enjoying the cool conditions. Give them as much light as you can up to about 50 per cent shade and keep them where they get air movement. Maintenance of a watering programme is necessary to ensure that they do not dry out. Many will have inflorescences well on their way.

Miltoniopsis should be in your heated glasshouse if you live in temperate areas. If in subtropical areas, a cool glasshouse should suffice. Remember that this is one genus that does not like extremes. It must be kept warm in winter and cool in summer.

Many growers of varicosum type oncidiums will have them in their winter rest spots, that is, somewhere where they can be kept away from cold winter rains but where they still receive good light. Do not try to keep them growing during this time, just let them enjoy a rest. This is what happens to them in nature. Temperatures down to freezing will not affect them unduly. A couple of sprays of water overhead in late August should wake them up for the next growing season.

September

Varicosum type oncidiums can be woken out of their winter dormancy now. Put them outside in the shadehouse. Root activity should soon start, together with new growth from the pseudobulbs. As roots progress and as the green tip lengthens, watering can be increased and feeding started. If they have to be divided or repotted, the first sign of root growth will indicate the appropriate stage. The new roots, which must not be damaged during the exercise, will then be able to go straight into the new mix or onto the new board without any setback.

Miltoniopsis and odontoglossums will need watching this month both for protection of flowers for those yet to finish this activity and for signs that the time is right for repotting. If you have an odontoglossum with a new growth 100 mm or so high, and it needs repotting, now is the time to do it. Miltoniopsis plants are still well and truly in their flowering cycle so it is best to leave repotting until the flowers are finished.

Fertilising can be resumed. Shading may have to be increased so as to ensure that the increasing light intensity does not set them back.

October–December

Varicosum type oncidiums in the shadehouse will enjoy all the light, water and feeding that you can give them. Keep pushing them along, as the longer and more intensive the growing season, the better the flowering will be early next year.

Oncidium River of Gold 'Susan Hughes' AD/NSW—easy to grow, easy to flower and very rewarding. Autumn is the main flush season. (OSNSW)

Wilsonara Zoe Stephenson. *Wilsonara* result from a cross between *Oncidium* and *Odontioda*. (Warren Gray)

Miltoniopsis Gordon Hoyt. These have an excellent ratio of flower production to pot size. (Warren Gray)

Oncidium forbesii 'Mum's Howler' HCC/NSW—an autumn-flowering Brazilian species of excellent shape and colour. (OSNSW)

Odontoglossums should be also in active growth. Repot as necessary and keep up your feeding activities. Never let them dry out. Some warm to hot weather will be experienced, so it is imperative that they be kept as cool as possible. A good balance between light intensity and cool conditions is necessary for ideal growth. Do not keep them too shaded as this will cause deep green leaves which, while they may look good, will be weak and thus susceptible to fungus infection. Also such growths give poor flowers later in the season.

Miltoniopsis plants will also be growing well now. Keep your heater primed in case there are cool nights and keep your evaporative cooler ready for the hot days which will be experienced. In some areas it can be possible, within a forty-eight-hour period, to have the need for heating *and* the need for cooling.

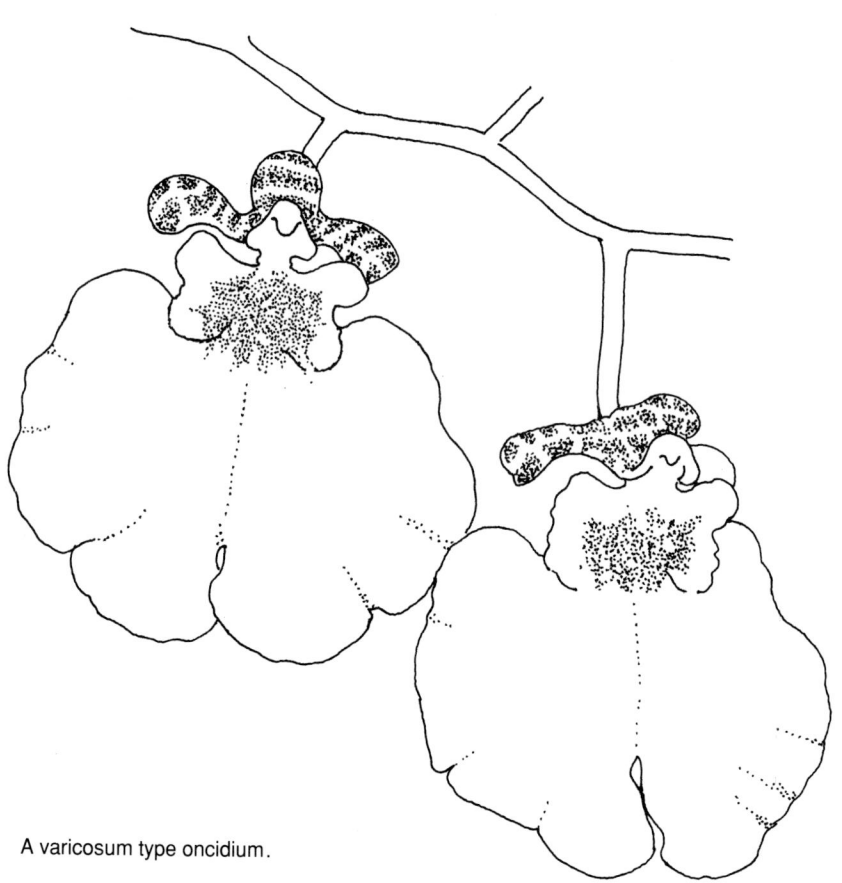

A varicosum type oncidium.

7. *Lycaste*

Lycaste is a genus of approximately twenty-five species found in Central America and the northern part of South America. They are essentially epiphytes (tree dwellers) and grow into large clumps, happily situated in forks of trees. Many also grow on rocks with their roots in tree litter. In their natural habitat they receive about 50–60 per cent shade throughout the year and have a more even day length than is the case in temperate areas. Yet the elevations at which they grow make them ideally suited for pot culture in subtropical and temperate areas. There are some species which need warmth in winter, however their specific needs will be well known to the specialist and the species growers.

This chapter is mainly concerned with one particular species and the hybrids developed from it over the decades since clones thereof first flowered in English glasshouses, or stovehouses as they were then known. The species is *Lycaste skinneri*. It has been virtually line-bred to produce an extensive array of attractive plants which make an imposing sight in the shadehouse, in the glasshouse, in the home and on the show bench. A check on the show results over the past decade or so will record many champion and grand champion awards to *Lycaste* hybrids.

Fifty per cent shade during the cooler months increasing to about 70 per cent in the warmer weather will suit them well. Shadehouse conditions year round from southern Queensland through to southern New South Wales will be in order, with some shelter required in Victoria and in South Australia mainly because of the need to maintain humidity around the plants. However, even where shadehouse conditions are acceptable, they do respond very well to glasshouse culture, providing that the light factor is maintained at the necessary levels.

Lycaste growers generally keep the plants moist all year with moderate to heavy watering during the period of active growth, say from October through until early autumn. During this growth cycle, fertilising as for cymbidiums is in order. In fact they love to be fed and will respond accordingly. Any good growing mix will suit them admirably, however it should be more on the fine side rather than medium and above. They will form an extensive root system if the mix is open but still retains moisture-holding capabilities.

As far as pests and diseases are concerned they are generally very hardy, however they can be affected by the usual orchid pests and diseases. There is a need to keep a close watch for problems and treat them accordingly.

Present-day hybrids, while predominantly of the *skinneri* type, have several species in their background and accordingly can flower at any time throughout the year. However, winter to early spring is the main season. Each inflorescence has only the one flower, but each bulb will have several such inflorescences so that a three- or four-bulb plant is capable of presenting a magnificent display—a real show stopper! Australia, through the hybridising activities of growers such as Fred Alcorn and John Apperley, both from New South Wales, is well to the fore in breeding of lycastes. As a consequence they are very popular plants in collections in this country. The ability of a well-grown and flowered plant to win at shows is an added feature. The only disadvantage they have is the size of the foliage. Leaves are very large and this means they require space to spread out in the shadehouse or glasshouse, otherwise they will overshadow plants around them. Consequently they are not conducive to inclusion in collections where growing space is limited.

Lycaste skinneri 'Sunbeam' HCC/NSW. This is a fine example of this popular species. Line breeding is greatly assisting the protection of existing wild populations. (OSNSW)

Lycaste Macama 'Radiance' AM/NSW. *Lycaste* hybridising has been progressing strongly in Australia for many years. This clone was from these efforts. (OSNSW)

Lycaste Koolena 'Elva' HCC/NSW. These are easily grown plants which do not require specialised conditions. (OSNSW)

Lycaste Shoalhaven 'Nowra' HCC/NSW—a spectacular plant to have in flower. Seedlings with similar potential are easily obtained. (OSNSW)

8. *Epidendrum/Encyclia*

We will deal here mainly with one loose grouping of these large and varied genera of exotic Central American orchids that are popular with landscape gardeners as well as with orchid people. There are more than 1000 species found in a wide range of climatic conditions. They form part of the very diverse *Oncidium* Alliance. Among the conspicuous features of the plants of this group are the bulbs and the leaves of the various species. Encyclias have plants with short, roundish bulbs topped with thin, narrow leaves, as well as those with bulbs up to 30 cm tall and 25 mm in diameter. Each bulb of this group is topped with two or three large, thick leaves. Altogether the plants have a similar appearance to cattleyas.

Epidendrums have tall, thin bulbs that have earned for them the name of 'reed-stems'. These bulbs may be as high as 1.5 m and no more than 25 mm in circumference. The stems of the plants of this group have alternate rows of light green, thick, firm leaves, 75 or 100 mm long by about 25 mm wide, that remain in good condition on the plants for several seasons. The leaves are about 65 mm apart in rows. They start near the base of the stem and continue up to where it starts to narrow and lengthen in preparation for producing a head of numerous star-shaped, long-lasting flowers approximately 25 mm wide. These are produced in succession for months at a time, even years in the case of some hybrids growing in ideal conditions. The individual flowers of the heads are presented upside down; thus the labellum is standing upright. The lip is three lobed, giving the upright labellum the appearance of a prominent miniature cross. Reed-stem epidendrums are often referred to as crucifix orchids because of these characteristics. Plants can be obtained with red, orange, lavender, yellow, pink, rose, fuschia, purple or white flowers. Many intermediate shades of these various colours are also to be found in the flowers.

Reed-stem epidendrums are popular. They are among the easiest of orchids to grow, if planted in sheltered, sunny positions away from heavy frost areas. Of this group there are both dwarf and tall-growing plants. The dwarf-growing species, which grow 60–90 cm tall, will make attractive specimens if planted in garden beds. They are also good plants for mass bedding or for pot cultivation. By breaking the rhizome (back-cutting), where possible, on established plants, they can be grown and multiplied within two or three years to produce up to twenty-five heads of flowers at one time. These plants can be kept in good condition and flowering at this rate for several years by pruning each stem back when the flower head has completely died.

If prolonged adverse weather conditions are experienced, the heads may temporarily cease flowering, and the buds may even drop, but if the tip of the stem remains alive, when ideal weather conditions return, buds show up again and flowers will again be produced. Often an offshoot will start another head of flowers. Do not be hasty with pruning as it may cost you flowers. When pruning is finally decided upon, cut the stem back to within about 100 mm of its base. This could cause a new, strong stem to start from near the base of the pruned stem, thus keeping the leading section strong, dwarf and young. All heads of flowers will not finish at the same time. By frequent pruning of plants needing attention a plant can be encouraged to produce many heads of flowers most of the time during ideal growing conditions. Some of the small growths which appear along the stem can be removed and potted up. They should flower within six months.

Mixing plants of several distinct colours in one small section of a flower bed or in a pot will make a pleasing arrangement. Be very sure when selecting pieces of plants for this work to get them from plants of similar height and growing habit.

The tall-growing plants (mixed colours) are good for growing in sunny positions in garden areas as low hedges or perhaps to hide some ugly background. Plant them alternately about 45 cm apart, in two or three rows, in a bed 60–90 cm wide. They will grow to about 1.5 m tall and flower there if grown, staked and trained correctly. If left alone the stems often send out aerial growths from near the top. These growths will raise the plants another foot or more in height and will flower. Such plantings, once established, need very little attention to keep them tidy and they give a brilliant show of flowers for a long time.

The pot growers should be planted in semi-terrestrial growing medium to which an additional 10 per cent of sharp sand is added. Plants growing in garden areas should be planted in light, rich, well-drained sandy loam.

Epidendrums are subject to attacks of fungus diseases; they are also attacked by insect and scale pests so they must be regularly checked for these problems.

They are easy to manage as far as moisture is concerned. Ideally, they should be kept fully moist, in well-drained soil, most of the time during the warm to hot months and reasonably dry much of the time during the cold winter months. Try not to cut the heads of flowers for vase work. It is better to pluck the individual flowers to use in shallow float bowls. They last well if supplied with cool, fresh water. Many florists use epidendrum flowers, even though small, in their 'make-up' work.

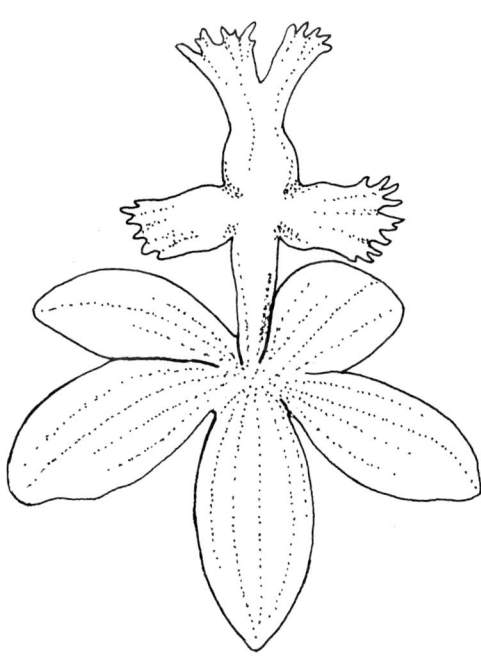

An individual epidendrum or crucifix orchid flower (enlarged).

Neolehmannia porpax 'Deanes' CC/NSW—a superb flowering of this unusual species, formerly known as *Epidendrum porpax*. The flowers resemble insects. (OSNSW)

Encyclia radiata 'Greta Maria' CC/NSW—a superb flowering of this easily grown species. (OSNSW)

9. *Phaius*

Phaius tankervilliae is a native orchid that is found growing in marshy areas around Brisbane and further north along the Queensland coastal areas. Like other native plants it is becoming scarcer each year as large tracts of land are cleared for farming and also because orchid plant collectors gather them. Its several long, erect, plaited, light green lanceolate leaves make a very handsome plant, even without flowers.

Phaius plants have often been brought as far south as Sydney, with the hope of growing them well in a shadehouse. As a rule, this does not happen. They only just 'make the grade' if grown in shadehouse conditions around Sydney. They certainly lose their handsome appearance. The tips of the leaves become black and ragged from dying back. Sometimes as much as half the leaf will be rotted away. This is a sure sign that the growing conditions are not right.

It is a pity to see any plant only just existing in adverse growing conditions, especially when such a plant is particularly handsome if well-grown. Our orchids are grown for the beauty they give us. We grow them to remind us of freshness, health and of loveliness. Half dead plants can only remind us of the exact opposite.

Phaius tankervilliae grows handsomely, and flowers regularly and well, in a glasshouse in a temperate zone where the temperature does not drop below about 10°C. Plants require a rich humus loam. They need a fair amount of shade (50 per cent Sydney sunlight) and to be kept very damp during the hot summer months when they are growing, and only just moist during the colder months when they are almost resting. Erect flower spikes will spring from the base of the new pseudobulbs. A strong spike will grow to a height of 1 m; flowers commence 45 cm from the top. The buds open in succession; one opens every third or fourth day. As there are up to a dozen blooms on a spike, each one lasting about ten days, there will be flowers on a plant for five or six weeks at a time. The flowers, which are about 10 cm wide when open, are fawn-coloured on the front of the sepals and petals and white on the reverse side. They usually bloom during late summer or early autumn.

The plants are a special target for mealy-bug and many other insect and scale pests.

Repot every second year when the new growth makes its appearance.

Other species of *Phaius* are found growing in certain parts of Africa and Asia. They all need warm glasshouse conditions in a temperate zone and all the other general growing requirements of *P. tankervilliae*. They all have the same handsome plants that produce lovely blooms in the brown-yellow tonings.

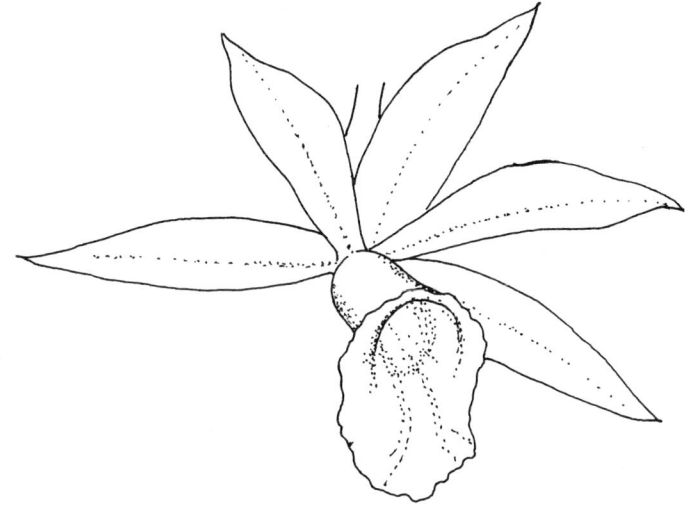

Phaius tankervilliae.

10. *Stanhopea*

Those familiar with orchids will recognise *Stanhopea* as that unusual genus which is always grown in a wire basket and whose flowers appear from the bottom of the basket. It originates in Central America. Its plants will grow exceedingly well and flower regularly in the warmer areas of the temperate regions. The plants need up to about 60 per cent shade, through a lattice, bramble or shadecloth roof, to produce good results. Each new pseudobulb is topped with a large, broad, plaited, dark green leaf. A plant of a dozen bulbs topped with their leaves is a very ornamental one. The highly scented flowers which may be up to 13 cm in diameter last from four to six days. The colour range of the flowers of the different species is from orange to dingy yellow, cream and white. Flowers of most of the species plants have many much darker coloured blotches and spots dotted or spread over them. The labellum is remarkably formed, being large, irregularly shaped, heavily formed and shiny as enamel.

Every orchid grower of several mixed genera should have some plants of this fascinating genus in his collection. So many of our cultivated orchids have very distinct habits for growing or producing their flowers. *Stanhopea* is one of these. It produces its flower scapes from the base of the bulbs and they grow downwards and are produced hanging perpendicularly, under the plant. In their natural habitat they overcome this 'disadvantage' by growing on the sides of trees, etc., covered with deep layers of moss, in which the roots ramble searching for food and moisture. The roots

Stanhopea wardii 'Jill' HCC/NSW—a fine example of this species. Stanhopeas are grown in baskets as the flowers push straight down from the plant. If grown in a pot, the flowers will be lost in the compost. (OSNSW)

Stanhopea anfracta 'Jill' HCC/NSW. Stanhopeas have a strong, sweet perfume. (OSNSW)

penetrate the moss and attach themselves to the outer firm surface of the plant's host, where they hold firm for years, even against storms and the weight from the bulk of a large plant.

The best methods for growing cultivated plants would be in shallow, wire baskets lined with long-lasting material which is easy to penetrate, such as paperbark, live moss from rocks, etc., or coconut fibre. The flower spike is quite thick so the wires in the basket should be no closer than 25 mm. Specimens are at times seen growing in baskets lined with bird wire. The spikes will not pass through such wire, so the plants never flower unless the spike is able to go over the top. Some species are less robust than others. Plants of these species could be mounted on the side of hanging slabs of open-grained treefern fibre.

The back-bulbs start young plants readily. In the early growing stages these young plants are grown in 100 or 125 mm pots, for easy cultivation and benching. To plant them in baskets immediately only serves to hasten the deterioration of the basket lining. Many of these plants are sold or exchanged at this early growing stage. Usually one is given strict instructions that when the plant nears flowering size it must be taken from the pot and planted in such a way that the scapes will have the opportunity to appear. This, of course, would not happen if they remained in a pot. Sometimes these instructions are not carried out. Make very sure that they are.

The plants should have an abundance of water during their summer growing months and should be kept fairly dry during the winter months, when they are just about dormant. For pot or basket cultivation they grow well in the semi-terrestrial orchid soil we recommend. For disease and pest control and fertilising, treat them the same as other orchid plants in the cymbidium section of the orchid house.

11. *Zygopetalum*

This is a small genus of orchids whose natural habitat is Central America. Some of its species are well worth growing as they have large, showy, fragrant flowers. The species *Zygopetalum mackayii* is extensively grown around the Sydney area. It is a pleasing orchid, even as a plant, to have in an orchid collection. It has oval, light green pseudobulbs which, when all the old sheaths are removed from them in the back-bulb stage, have the appearance in shape, colour and size of large, light green plums. A growth starts developing in late spring and by early autumn it is well advanced but not filled out to form a bulb.

In early autumn, the growth, if it is going to flower, will send up a spike, from near the base, between the leaves of the new growth. This spike will grow and develop rather quickly and should be about 60 cm tall and flowering within eight weeks from when it was first visible. It should produce from four to seven flowers each of about 65 mm in diameter.

The sepals and petals are a dull, light green with many distinct chocolate-coloured patches dotted over them. The 35 mm broad, flat lip of the labellum is most striking in appearance. Its main colour is white. This is patterned with many purplish blue broken lines. The flowers are heavily and pleasingly perfumed (perhaps with a strong wisteria scent).

The flowers should last for a month or more if cared for correctly. That is, the plant should be watered regularly, also it should be kept in the cool section of the flowering house, where the flowers would be protected from any adverse weather conditions. They make excellent cut flowers.

As the plant is flowering and after the flowers are finished, the growth continues to develop until a bulb is grown and the season's cycle is completed. Each new bulb is topped with three or four lanceolate, light green leaves about 380 mm long and 35 mm wide. The plants defoliate earlier than do the cymbidium plants. They grow well and flower regularly each year if they are grown in the shadier, warmer parts of the cymbidium house. If grown under conditions which are too cool or too damp, the slightly soft leaves seem to develop many smallish black spots; also the plants defoliate earlier than normal.

For general cultivation, use the cymbidium potting mix and practise the cymbidium cultural notes. However, care must be exercised with the watering of the plants while the new growths are young. If water rests in a new growth, it (together with any young flower spikes) can easily be lost through central growth rot.

The zygopetalum plants are harder to establish after division than cymbidiums. September is a very good month to divide or recondition any plants that need attention. Most roots on the back-bulbs remain in good condition for several years after the leaves have fallen. When intending to use the back-bulbs for propagation purposes it is better to back-cut them some time during the first September after they have turned into back-bulbs. The back-cut back-bulbs will establish strong, young plants readily this way. These plants may be potted out into their own pots at next reconditioning time.

Sometimes other species of this genus can be purchased. Some of these flower during late summer while others flower in mid-winter. By selecting varied species, flowering zygopetalum plants can be on the orchid benches for several months each year. Most of them will flourish well if given similar cultural treatment to *Zygopetalum mackayii*.

Zygopetalum Artur Elle 'Stonehurst' AM/NSW. Zygopetalums grow easily with cymbidiums. (OSNSW)

12. Vandaceous Types

This general section loosely covers all of the orchids that have vandaceous type growth, that is, those that are monopodial in their habit. There are two types of growth in orchids, sympodial (where the plant puts out new bulbs from the base as it 'creeps' across a pot or up the side of a host tree, etc.) and monopodial (where the plant's growth follows a continuous upward trend, that is, it just keeps growing up and up). *Vanda* species obviously fall into the latter category, however closely related genera, such as *Aerides*, *Ascocentrum*, *Renanthera*, *Arachnis*, *Phalaenopsis* and *Angraecum*, also have monopodial growth.

Right: Ascocenda Meda Arnold 'Daphne' AM/NSW. The combining of *Vanda* and *Ascocentrum* has resulted in small-growing plants with intense colour. (OSNSW)

Vanda Hilo Blue 'Nesnah' HCC-AD/NSW. Vandas require a lot of light to flower well. (OSNSW)

These have, as a general rule, spectacular and colourful flowers and some of the gems of the orchid world are to be found amongst them. In tropical areas they grow almost like weeds. Anyone who has seen the vandas growing in the Singapore Gardens will appreciate this statement. They are to be found growing in full sun where they flower profusely. In subtropical areas some warmth during the winter helps. In temperate areas, this is a must with most types (a few exceptions will be noted later in this chapter).

Watering and feeding regularly are essential for good growth, in view of the fact that they generally originate from low elevations in tropical areas where growth is almost continuous year around. They are heavy feeders and in this regard can be treated virtually the same as cymbidiums. High humidity is necessary.

Except for *Phalaenopsis* and its ilk, it is in the area of light that most problems arise for growers in subtropical and temperate areas. As mentioned they can take a lot of light, with the terete-leaved types (the Singapore Gardens ones) taking full tropical sun very easily. Away from the tropics it is difficult to provide the same light intensity throughout the year, the differential between day length and night length increasing sharply the further south one goes. Even in the case of plants grown under clear glass, in winter time they will not receive the amount of light required for good growth and, as a consequence, good flowering. In temperate areas they are, as a general rule, marginal subjects only, to be left to the specialist growers.

Vanda coerulea is a very popular species, being of a delightful blue colouring. This is a colour not often found in the orchid world. There is an added benefit in that it is found in nature growing at high elevations. As a consequence it is more adaptable to culture in temperate areas than its tropical cousins. Lack of light intensity in the cooler months is, however, still a major problem. This species is widely grown, but it is in the area of hybridising that its presence has been well and truly beneficial. Crossed with the tropical types it has given a range of colours not previously available to temperate area growers. *Ascocenda (Vanda × Ascocentrum)* is an example of this development.

A typical phalaenopsis bloom with its symmetrical rounded shape and pure white colour. These are very popular for wedding bouquets. (Warren Gray)

Phalaenopsis plants in bloom at Bryant's Nursery, Kurnell NSW. Phalaenopsis are warm-growing orchids. They like relatively high humidity and low light. They may be grown successfully indoors under a fluorescent tube or near a lightly curtained window in the right aspect. (Warren Gray)

Vanda, *Phalaenopsis* and *Renanthera* have very strong root systems. The roots are large and fleshy and they are very difficult to keep confined to a pot. Large-sized bark chunks are ideal as this medium allows the roots to ramble freely, however many will decide that they prefer life outside the pot to that inside. Some growers actually place the plants in completely empty pots allowing the plants to clamber as they will. This requires careful maintenance of correct watering and humidity. Good drainage is essential as they are true epiphytes.

Phalaenopsis plants require shadier conditions than their vandaceous cousins. Leaf growth has adapted to the heavy shade of rainforest conditions so they are more at home with the light level required by say paphiopedilums (refer to Chapter 3). They have, otherwise, the same requirements as regards water, feeding, warmth and humidity as the others. Because of their low light requirements, they can be adapted to indoor culture. All they need is a light and airy position and some humidity (plus being kept moist of course) and they will grow and flower reasonably well, although they will not be as good as glasshouse-grown examples. A temperature of 12°C is about as low as they should experience for best results. The higher the minimum, the better the results.

Because of the nature of their growth, the vandaceous types are difficult to propagate. At times, off-shoots will develop and, as plants elongate, it is possible on occasions to cut away the top (with a few roots). This part will continue to grow, and the piece left in the pot will send out one or more new off-shoots. It is still a very slow process.

Vandaceous types do not have any definite rest period, the same conditions virtually being required all year. However, at time of flowering, which can be at any time of the year, the root growth seems to be reduced somewhat, so a slight reduction in watering and feeding is desirable. Otherwise, no damage will be incurred if they are treated just the same as the other plants in the house.

Pests and diseases are attracted to them just as they are to any other orchid and the general control methods should be followed.

Phalaenopsis Devon Michele 'Syd Collins'. This is a well-shaped semi-alba. (Warren Gray)

Vanda Gordon Dillon 'Homestead' HCC/NSW. Vandas require warmth in winter for successful cultivation in the southern States. (OSNSW)

Phalaenopsis (Paifang's Queen × Ella Danseuse)—a candy-striped variety that has heavy substance. (Warren Gray)

Phalaenopsis unknown 'Julie-Ann'. This shows a very pleasing presentation. (Warren Gray)

Phalaenopsis ([Zadazu × Kathleen Voelker] × Lippepracht) 'Kurnell'. This exhibits an excellent shape. (Warren Gray)

13. Species Orchids

In excess of 25 000 species of orchids are recognised. Their habitats range from high in the mountains to sea level, from cold to tropical conditions and they grow on or in trees, rocks or earth and some even grow virtually in the air having only the minimum of attachment to the tree or rock or whatever. Some have tuberoids, some have pseudobulbs, some do not have any bulbs at all, some do not have leaves. Some have sympodial growth (new growths appear from base of the plant) whereas others are monopodial (they just keep growing up and up).

Obviously it is just not possible to give general cultural requirements for all these different kinds of orchids because, even within the one genus, individual species will have adapted to specific climatic and habitat conditions. A dedicated grower of species orchids will endeavour to provide as wide a range of environments as possible, using shadehouse and cold and heated glasshouse areas, moving plants as necessary until a spot is found where they appear to be happy.

Species orchids, particularly those from tropical areas, started the interest in orchids in the early 1700s. This interest increased until it reached its peak in the mid- to late 1800s. During the heyday of orchid collecting, when special trips were commissioned by the large orchid nurseries of the day, hundreds of thousands of plants found their way to Europe. This trade obviously had some effect on the world populations and some species were placed in jeopardy. However, by far the major cause of the orchid conservation problems is the habitat destruction that has, in many areas, been progressing virtually out of control for decades. This habitat destruction has caused the extinction of many species. The process continues even as the 1990s approach, yet, for bureaucratic quarantine reasons, many of the plants that are left to die or to be burnt cannot be sent to areas (Australia, for example) where their continued existence could be assured by being in the care of orchid enthusiasts across the country.

Most orchid growers fully accept the need to conserve species. If this is not possible as far as wild populations are concerned, then certainly it can be done artificially by the propagation of species and their subsequent distribution to many growers. Specialist orchid societies have been formed and these societies have as one of their aims, the raising of seedlings, particularly of scarce or endangered species. The Australian Orchid Foundation conducts a seed bank where growers undertake selfings or sibling crosses* of species and forward the resultant seed to the seed bank. It is then distributed to growers both in Australia and worldwide. The Curator's address is 66 Ethel St, Sanctuary Point NSW 2540.

Specialist growers certainly contribute to the survival of many species. The following is a brief listing of the species that can be found in flower, during the months mentioned, having been grown in the houses listed in an area such as Sydney. Further north some will flower earlier and will require less warmth and care, whereas further south a shadehouse subject may require a cold glasshouse. Even within a species some clones will be more adaptable than others.

* Selfings result when two flowers from the same clone are used to obtain seed. Sibling crosses are when two flowers of the same species or hybrid, but from different clones, are used.

Breeding orchids requires skill and patience. The first step is pollination, placing the pollen from one flower on the stigma of another. When fertilisation takes place, a seed pod develops. In approximately six months, the seed is ready to be sown in a flask, on a surface composed of agar jelly and chemical compounds. When the new plants are large enough, they are placed in community pots, and later, when 8–10 cm high, they should be moved into single 10 cm pots. (Warren Gray)

Community pots of cymbidium. (Warren Gray)

Catasetum Orchidglade 'Orchidglade II' AM/NSW. This is not the easiest of subjects to grow, however the flowers are very spectacular. These are male flowers. Hybridists are now very active with many of the lesser known genera. *Catasetum* hybrids are an example of what is being achieved in this regard. The new hybrids are so many and varied that it is just not possible to specifically cover each type in a publication such as this. Membership of an orchid society will enable growers to pose cultural queries to the experts. (OSNSW).

Brassia verrucosa 'Greta Maria' CC/NSW—an easily grown and heavily perfumed South American species. (OSNSW)

Coelogyne flaccida 'Mt Ford' CC/NSW—easily grown and highly fragrant. A show stopper when well flowered. (OSNSW)

Dendrobium kingianum 'Bungan Castle' AM-CC/NSW—one of the easiest of all Australian natives to grow and flower. (OSNSW)

January	Shadehouse	*Anguloa clowesii* *Disa tripetaloides* *Maxillaria tenuifolia* *Stanhopea nigroviolacea*
	Cool glasshouse	*Encyclia adenocaula* *Encyclia alata* *Mormolyca ringens* *Sarcochilus ceciliae*
February	Shadehouse	*Brassavola tuberculata* *Lycaste aromatica* *Stanhopea occulata* *Vanda coerulea*
	Cool glasshouse	*Brassavola nodosa* *Bulbophyllum rothschildianum* *Encyclia cochleata*
	Heated glasshouse	*Cattleya bicolor* *Doritis pulcherrima*
March	Shadehouse	*Dendrochilum cobbianum* *Lycaste deppei* *Miltonia spectabilis* *Oncidium flexuosum*
	Cool glasshouse	*Dendrobium lawesii* *Gongora galeata* *Masdevallia veitchiana* *Sophronitis coccinea*
	Heated glasshouse	*Dendrobium bigibbum* *Phalaenopsis violacea*
April	Shadehouse	*Coelogyne ovalis* *Oncidium enderianum* *Oncidium varicosum* *Rossioglossum grande* *Zygopetalum mackayii*
	Cool glasshouse	*Cattleya bowringiana* *Laelia pumila* *Neolehmannia porpax* *Paphiopedilum charlesworthii*
	Heated glasshouse	*Catasetum pileatum*
May	Shadehouse	*Cymbidium tracyanum* *Laelia anceps* *Laelia autumnalis* *Laelia gouldiana* *Liparis reflexa*

May	Cool glasshouse	*Coelogyne speciosa* *Liparis viridiflora* *Paphiopedilum gratrixianum* *Paphiopedilum insigne*
	Heated glasshouse	*Paphiopedilum haynaldianum* *Phalaenopsis cornucervi* *Trichoglottis philippinensis*
June	Shadehouse	*Bulbophyllum macphersonii* *Dendrobium monophyllum* *Oncidium ornithorhynchum*
	Cool glasshouse	*Calanthe vestita* *Paphiopedilum fairrieanum* *Paphiopedilum spicerianum* *Paphiopedilum villosum*
	Heated glasshouse	*Bulbophyllum medusae* *Rhynchostylis gigantea* *Sophronitis cernua*
July	Shadehouse	*Bulbophyllum bracteatum* *Vanda teres*
	Cool glasshouse	*Maxillaria variabilis* *Osmoglossum pulchellum* *Paphiopedilum callosum*
	Heated glasshouse	*Angraecum eburneum* *Ludisia discolor* *Rhyncholaelia glauca*
August	Shadehouse	*Aerides vandarum* *Coelogyne flaccida* *Dendrobium aemulum* *Dendrobium teretifolium* *Maxillaria porphyrostele*
	Cool glasshouse	*Encyclia fragrans* *Odontoglossum crispum* *Maxillaria densa*
	Heated glasshouse	*Coelogyne pandurata* *Phalaenopsis schilleriana*
September	Shadehouse	*Cattleya loddigesii* *Coelogyne cristata* *Dendrobium kingianum* *Dendrobium loddigesii* *Dendrobium pierardii* *Dendrobium primulinum* *Pterostylis baptistii*

Dendrobium teretifolium 'Eden Leigh' CC/NSW—a spectacular Australian native orchid. (OSNSW)

Dendrobium pierardii 'Fred' CC/NSW—a species that rewards its owner with a profusion of flowers in spring. (OSNSW)

Arpophyllum spicatum 'Bexley' CC/NSW—a suitable subject for shadehouse culture from Sydney north. Previously known as *Arpophyllum giganteum*. (OSNSW)

September	Cool glasshouse	*Arpophyllum spicatum*
		Leptotes bicolor
		Maxillaria picta
		Pleione formosana
	Heated glasshouse	*Epidendrum pseudepidendrum*
October	Shadehouse	*Cymbidium devonianum*
		Cymbidium madidum
		Cymbidium suave
		Dendrobium chrysotoxum
		Dendrobium farmeri
		Dendrobium griffithianum
		Dendrobium nobile
		Phaius tankervilliae
		Sarcochilus hartmannii
	Cool glasshouse	*Cymbidium canaliculatum*
		Laelia harpophylla
		Laelia purpurata
November	Shadehouse	*Bifrenaria harrisonae*
		Brassia verrucosa
		Coelogyne massangeana
		Dendrobium densiflorum
		Dendrobium fimbriatum
		Neobenthamia gracilis
		Polystachya pubescens
	Cool glasshouse	*Ansellia africana*
		Bifrenaria tetragona
		Dendrobium sanderae
		Encyclia mariae
	Heated glasshouse	*Phragmipedium caudatum*
		Dendrobium trigonopus
December	Shadehouse	*Calanthe triplicata*
		Disa uniflora
		Laelia tenebrosa
		Oncidium sarcodes
		Stanhopea tigrina
		Thunia marshalliana
	Cool glasshouse	*Mystacidium capense*
		Nageliella purpurea
		Neofinetia falcata
	Heated glasshouse	*Aeranthes grandiflora*
		Angraecum magdalenae
		Oncidium onustum
		Paphiopedilum hookerae

Index